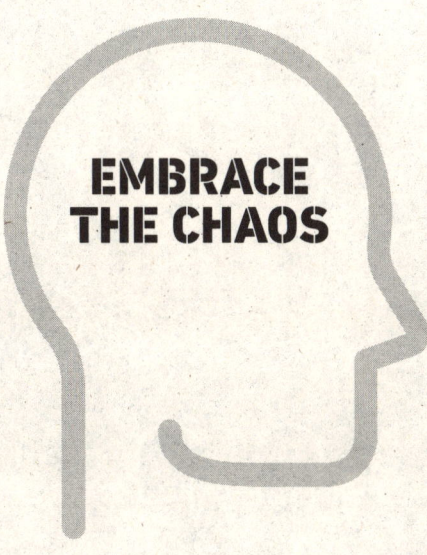

EMBRACE
THE CHAOS

www.penguin.co.uk

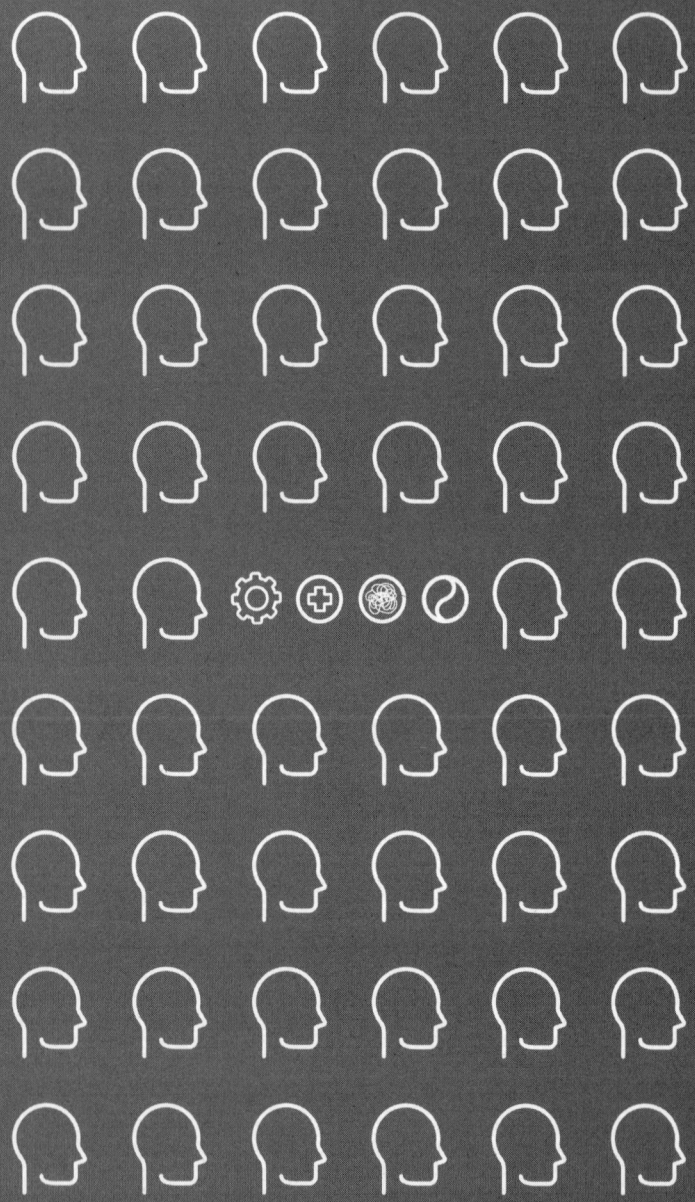

EMBRACE THE CHAOS

52 TACTICS TO MAKE EVERY DAY COUNT

BY
JASON FOX
WITH
MATT ALLEN

PENGUIN BOOKS

TRANSWORLD PUBLISHERS
Penguin Random House, One Embassy Gardens,
8 Viaduct Gardens, London SW11 7BW
www.penguin.co.uk

Transworld is part of the Penguin Random House group of companies
whose addresses can be found at global.penguinrandomhouse.com

First published in Great Britain in 2024 by Bantam
an imprint of Transworld Publishers
Penguin paperback edition published 2025

A CIP catalogue record for this book
is available from the British Library.

ISBN
9781804991527

Designed by Bobby Birchall, Bobby&Co
Typeset in Din Next Pro regular
Printed and bound in India by Thomson Press India Ltd.

The authorized representative in the EEA is Penguin Random House Ireland,
Morrison Chambers, 32 Nassau Street, Dublin D02 YH68.

To my parents, Peter and Hilary, two people who really have had a journey through life. They've ridden the highs and dug deep during the lows. To complicate matters, they've raised three hectic lads pretty well.

To them, and everyone out there riding their own highs and lows, remember to always embrace the chaos.

CONTENTS

PART TWO: RECOVERY

PART THREE: CHAOS

PART FOUR: CALM

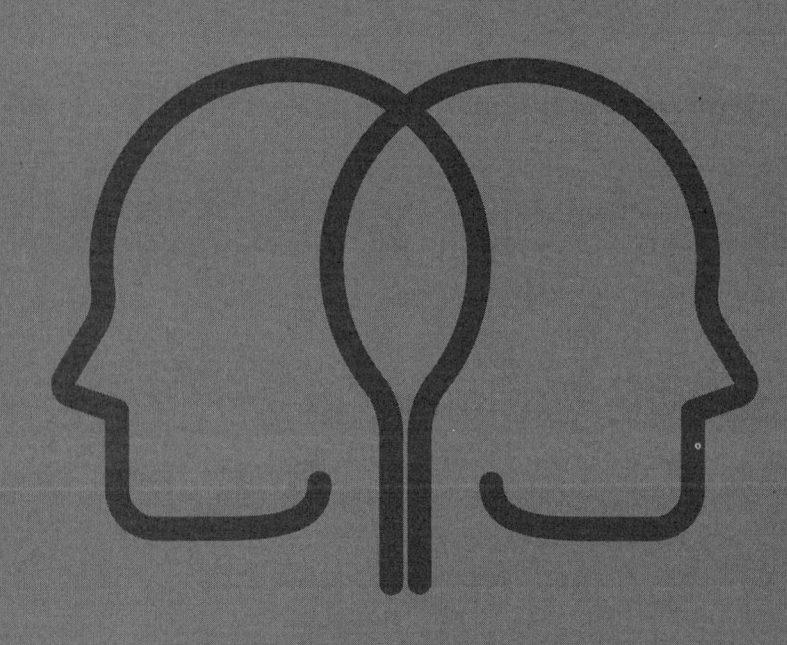

INTRODUCTION

LOCATION: CULIACAN, MEXICO; AN AREA KNOWN AS 'EL CHAPO'S BACKYARD'

DATE: WINTER 2018

In a small, dingy bungalow, I stood face to face with three lieu-
tenants from the Sinaloa cartel, one of the world's most terrifying drug gangs. Their identities had been disguised with black
balaclavas – each one bearing an intimidating skull design on the
front – but I could see their eyes; they were bloodshot, probably
due to the rails of cocaine that each one had noisily inhaled upon
arriving. I could also see their guns: all three men had stuffed a
Glock into the waistband of their jeans and it had been announced
that a stash of automatic weapons was placed somewhere nearby.
Being heavily tooled up was a job requirement when working for a
murderous organization like the Sinaloa gang.

I'd found myself in this edgy situation thanks to the mechanics
of TV production. At the time, I was making a documentary series
for Channel 4 called *Meet the Drug Lords: Inside the Real Narcos*,
for which I'd been asked to interview a number of serious players from the Mexican and Colombian cocaine racket. A fixer had
arranged for a camera crew and me to meet with El Chapo's mob,
but immediately I'd got the sense that we might have bitten off
more than we could chew. Our meeting point was in the badlands,
and when we heard a knock on the door I was the only one who
seemed willing to open it – the others were already cowering behind a kitchen counter.

Bloody hell, I thought. *I'll do it, then.*

I peered into the street outside and my heart sank: there was no one there. *Was this a come-on?* I even flinched at the expectation of a sudden *bup-bup-bup* of machine-gun fire, but nothing moved. The only sound was the chatter of cicadas . . . And then three armed men stepped out from the shadows.

The Sinaloa cartel had brought an interpreter along with them, as had we, but theirs arrived with demands.

'There will be no questions about other people in the cartel,' he said, as everyone gathered inside. 'You will not ask about the hierarchy of the cartel, or the leadership . . .'

The list went on, but their interpreter looked unsettled. He seemed just as nervous as we were, which wasn't a good sign, and when the filming began, he stammered and blundered his way through the first round of questions. From what I could tell, he was asking all the questions that had been declared off-limits, rather than translating what I was saying. *Was he so scared that he could only focus on the things we'd been warned against discussing?* It certainly seemed that way, because he was blurting everything out in a weird panic. Then the scene turned ugly.

'Right! Stop there!' the lead hit-man shouted at us. 'If any of you fucks says anything like that again, I'm going to pull this weapon out and kill you right here. Then we'll bury you in the desert.'

I took a breath. Having previously experienced being tangled up in conflict situations where two opposing groups with raised weapons were unable to speak the language of the other, I understood the importance of someone taking charge. Rather than trying to pacify anyone, I treated the scenario as a military event and instructed both sides on what needed to be done. Through our interpreter, I told the gunmen that there had been a misunderstanding – we wouldn't be asking any hostile questions. I then suggested their interpreter translated my questions exactly – word for word, with no screwing around.

Was I shitting myself? A little bit. But by taking charge of the variables that were under my control, I'd found the emotional strength to stay calm and negotiate in what was potentially a brutal final act for my team and me. The end result was an intense interview, but the mood had undoubtedly softened. Before they left, the lads from Sinaloa offered us a sample of their product, by way of a toast. I thanked them diplomatically, but declined.

Psychological strategies of that kind were very much the stock in trade for me while scrapping at the sharp point of war with the British military elite. I was part of a group that moved with autonomy, capable of thinking outside the box and willing to improvise when the odds of survival were stacked against us. Happy to serve as both team leaders and team players, our job was to raise the bar in combat and this was done by utilizing new techniques, game-changing technologies and innovative ideas. Every life-or-death event was faced with expertly-thought-out strategy. And if a battle plan for the task ahead hadn't been put in place already, we would devise one on the fly, learning from our victories and defeats as we progressed, so that our groundbreaking new tactics could be either improved for the next raid or struck off as being too hazardous to attempt again.

As a military asset, I was a highly effective tool, more skeleton key than blunt instrument, and the skills developed and advanced by those of us serving in the top tier would later prove transferable to the real world. This was because the British Armed Forces had learned that war cycled through really only four phases – Mission (or performance), Recovery, Chaos (or survival) and Calm – and a number of relevant processes and tactics were established so that every individual could thrive and survive within them. On the surface, the use of these four categories may have seemed a very simplistic way of viewing our overly complicated day-to-day existences, but, really, they were easy to understand because they reflected just about everyone's daily experience one way or another. When viewed honestly, it was fairly clear that the stages of Mission, Recovery, Chaos and Calm were applicable to just about any walk of life.

So, for example:

MISSION

A challenge, and one that might present itself in all manner of ways. It might be driving lessons, starting a family, retraining, learning a new language, rehab from addiction, walking from Land's End to John O'Groats, overcoming a phobia, running a first marathon, chemotherapy, studying for a degree, developing a start-up idea, getting married, and so on . . . If we're to succeed in an event of this kind, we need to be mentally and physically ready. Preparation and perseverance is key, as is positivity. The weak-minded and ill-prepared will perform poorly or fail.

RECOVERY

A period of learning. It's in the Recovery phase that an individual can regroup from a mission or challenge, both in a personal sense and as part of any collective effort that may have taken place. Intelligence and insights from that mission are collected and discussed, new targets and goals are worked upon, and time is taken to recuperate physically and emotionally, so that when the next test arrives we can feel prepared for another period of intense work.

CHAOS

Periods of manic energy, stress, worry, frustration and strained emotion. This cycle can arrive in all manner of ways. At the milder end of the spectrum, maybe we've missed the bus for a job interview. Or perhaps an unwanted commitment has landed in our lap, like a period of jury service. More extreme events such as family bereavement, the collapse of a relationship or a traumatic injury can upend us to the point where we can't think clearly. In chaotic situations such as these, our fight-or-flight mechanisms are engaged, compelling the body and mind to work to their maximum. The effort to keep our heads above water is gruelling. It's also unsustainable if we're not familiar with managing a hefty workload in such an emotional state.

CALM

We're knackered, blown out by the emotional stress or physical fatigue (or both) experienced in the Chaos phase: maybe we've worked way too hard, or perhaps the emotional aftermath of dealing with missed buses, jury service commitments, bereavement or painful psychological injuries has left us feeling shot, burned out and frayed around the edges. When the main source of our stress eventually fades, we're still prone to emotional outbursts, and the body aches. Life feels like a rollercoaster and there's no way of getting off. In these moments, it's important we use the Calm phase to regroup and learn, so that the issues that led us to chaos won't derail us again – or we can find time to plan and prepare more effectively for our next Mission phase.

If we are to view our lives through these four phases, it's fairly easy to see how most events fall into their clearly defined patterns. And it's this cycle of phases that makes up the heartbeat of *Embrace the Chaos: 52 Tactics to Make Every Day Count*. As an elite operator, I was trained to cope with the churn of Mission, Recovery, Chaos and Calm during combat. When operations popped up, which they did on an almost nightly basis, I knew to prepare as best I could for them by planning the work ahead in detail, squaring away my personal admin and understanding exactly what was required of me when the scrapping started. During the Recovery phase, the team would debrief and learn from any mistakes we'd made, because assessing the intelligence we'd gathered, and considering how it might affect future efforts, was a valuable process. During Chaos, I understood how to manage my physical workload and psychological state for when people were shooting at me and my teammates were dying. In moments of Calm, I knew how to rest my mind and body in order to be prepared for the next mission, and I'd take on new courses and learn different skills so I could return to battle an even more effective operator than before.

I also discovered the consequences of *not* managing these four cycles effectively. As my military career drew to a close, I became emotionally frazzled in what was an endless cycle of horrific violence. As a result, I lost sight of what needed to be done during the Calm and Recovery phases. Chaos became my default setting, until I eventually quit the military and hit rock bottom, landing at a point where suicide seemed like my only escape from a world of never-ending hurt. Thankfully, after a period of intervention from friends, therapy eventually restored balance and saved my life.

The upshot of this brutal experience was that I soon learned to work through the phases of Mission, Recovery, Chaos and Calm away from the theatre of combat. In the process, I built a fitter, happier and more productive experience for myself, one that now feels loaded with purpose and new friendships, challenges and rewards. I discovered how to manage the emotional pressures that so nearly killed me. I set myself inspiring tests and challenges, and spent time learning from the successes I'd enjoyed, or from any mistakes that may have prevented me from hitting my goals. More importantly, I discovered that the strategies I'd been using to hit this rewarding equilibrium were transferable to all manner of everyday events and lifestyles, no matter how unique and disruptive they may appear in the moment.

Embrace the Chaos: 52 Tactics to Make Every Day Count distils these strategies into easily executed actions, practices or thought processes. And in many ways it represents the third and final phase in a trio of books in which I've dealt with the vitally important issues of mental health, emotional resilience and psychological well-being. *Battle Scars: A Story of War and All That Follows* was a case study for a life spent in combat and its aftermath. *Life Under Fire: How to Build Inner Strength and Thrive Under Pressure* was rooted in theory, one that revealed the mindset required to attain emotional balance. *Embrace the Chaos: 52 Tactics to Make Every Day Count* is the practical endgame and details a series of instantly actionable plans for when operating in those familiar cycles of Mission, Recovery, Chaos and Calm.

Split into four sections of thirteen chapters each, the book breaks down the skills required to thrive – or endure – within each cycle. The numbers 52 and 13 are by no means arbitrary choices: *Embrace the Chaos: 52 Tactics to Make Every Day Count* can be read from cover to cover, or its techniques can be tried out on a weekly basis – or the reader can randomize the experience by picking from a deck of ordinary playing cards and then working from the marked, corresponding chapter. (See the appendix on p. 258.) Each chapter will deliver anecdotes and experiences from both my military and non-military careers, as examples of how the techniques have been battle-tested. Within each lesson, the various techniques that can be applied are laid out along with some necessary practical steps the reader can take to experience substantial personal progress.

Life is turbulent. It ebbs and flows in ways that we sometimes fail to manage or maximize, but with the right training it is possible to negotiate its four main cycles – Mission, Recovery, Chaos and Calm – effectively, so that we can grow stronger and more resilient, no matter the challenges thrown our way. During my military career I worked like a Swiss Army knife, a versatile asset capable of overcoming all sorts of challenges. By absorbing the techniques distilled in *Embrace the Chaos: 52 Tactics to Make Every Day Count*, you can become the same.

Foxy
London, 2024

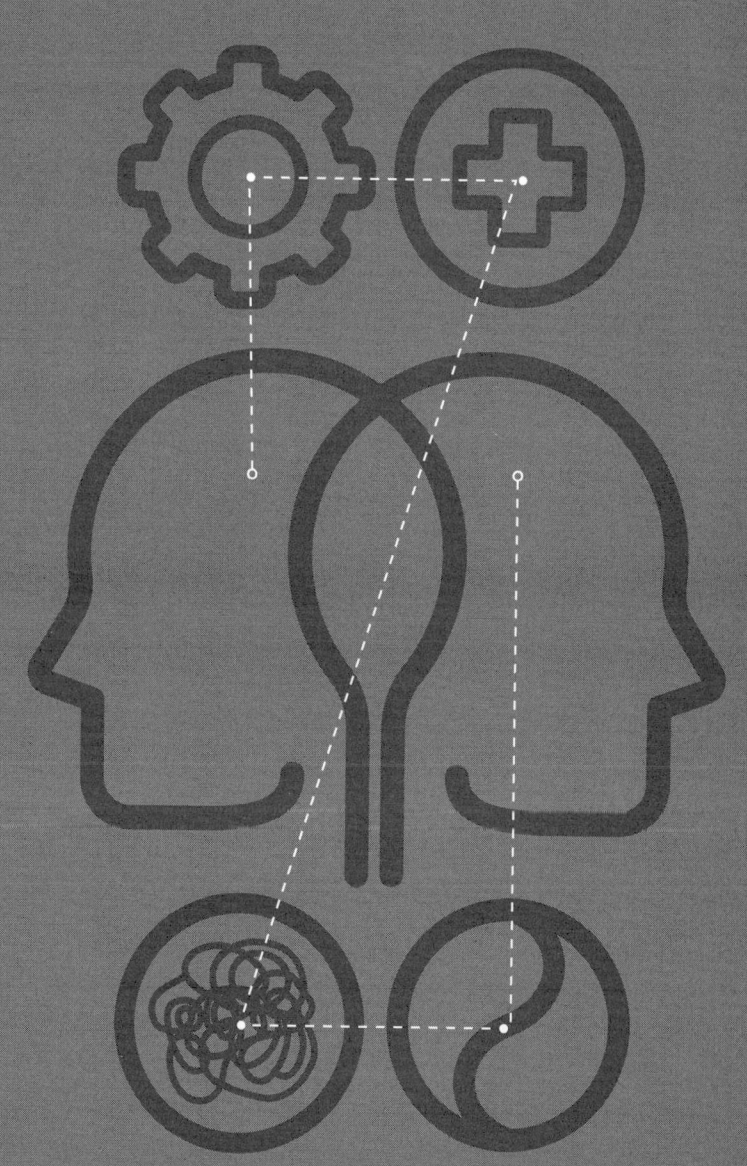

PART ONE:
MISSION

INTRODUCTION

WHAT IS A MISSION?

In a literal sense, the term represents an arduous challenge that takes place over an extended period of time, like a trek across a treacherous landscape such as a mountainous region or a jungle. But in reality, it can be anything that tests a person physically, mentally or emotionally – or everything at once. What isn't explained is that every mission is an opportunity, one that forces the participating individual into successive moments of fear and discomfort that need to be faced head-on in order to succeed. Once the mission or challenge has been completed successfully (or unsuccessfully, in some cases) the individual or individuals involved will nearly always feel an expanded sense of well-being and personal growth, especially if they've been pushed to their limits and learned from the experience. In other words: *cracking a mission will make you feel very good about yourself.*

All of this is easier said than done, though, and the very thought of taking on a difficult task can be stressful. (It's also a good thing *not* having to deal with fear and discomfort.) We all love a night on the sofa with our significant other, or a day in the pub with mates, plus those trips to a favourite restaurant, football ground or museum. We love our comfortable lives. *But where's the challenge in any of that?* When we're not pushing our personal boundaries we're stagnating, and that lack of growth can result in a loss of purpose. In very low moments, our self-respect can take a kicking, too.

For example, many relationships crumble when one or both partners lose their desire to attempt new challenges, or to experience adventures together. The love might still be there, but things

feel stale because the brakes have been pumped on any exciting growth. Facing an obstacle as a partnership is sometimes the perfect way to escape that sense of stasis because it tends to deliver a jolt to the senses. Even a small test, like planning a holiday together, can be enough to jump-start things again.

So where are you in your life right now? Do you have a sense of purpose, or are you stuck in a rut? It might be that you're actively looking for something to take you out of your comfort zone, such as a physical or mental challenge. Or maybe life has thrust you into a position where you're suddenly required to learn different techniques, take on greater responsibilities or thrive under pressure. Either way, you've embarked on a mission, or been pushed into one (whether you know it or not), and the very first step in succeeding is to treat it as such – *no excuses*.

Nailing the job won't be easy, though. Missions aren't supposed to be cakewalks. But over the coming pages I'm going to present you with an armoury of skills and procedures that should provide tactical support as you prepare, execute and grow into your challenge, whether you're climbing a mountain, organizing a charity drive, learning a new language, or having your very first kid. Of course, 100 per cent success isn't guaranteed – nothing in life ever is. But by following my advice you'll give yourself a greater chance of bomb-proofing your progress without wandering into any psychological booby traps.

CHAPTER 1
DEFINE YOUR CHALLENGE

Life is a succession of missions, and experience has taught me that there are generally two types: the *proactive* and the *reactive*. In a military context, a proactive operation is generally conducted on your side's terms, such as a strike on a hostile group. A reactive operation, meanwhile, is an immediate response to an unforeseen situation, like the enemy's use of some unexpected tactic or an ambush on your position. In a non-military setting, examples of proactive missions might include physical and educational challenges, sponsorship drives and personal projects. Reactive missions are usually challenges that strike out of nowhere, such as a serious illness or injury, or surprising and pressurized life events like a forced job relocation or an unexpected pregnancy.

Firstly, it's worth saying that nobody can really prepare fully for a reactive event – they're usually shocking by nature. Proactive missions, however, *can* be mapped out and trained for, so when selecting one it's important to think carefully about what it is that you want to do, especially if personal growth is the ultimate aim. Say you're hoping to shift some weight. There's no point taking on a 10K run if training in the pissing wet for months on end is going to leave you feeling miserable and demoralized. There's every chance you'll quit. Instead, consider your personal requirements when researching a potential challenge. These should be motivating factors to ensure you remain committed to the task. My checklist usually includes:

- Time spent in nature.
- A physical challenge.
- Something that will put the shits up me.
- Brotherhood (time with mates).

What mission you choose is entirely up to you of course, but in the past five years or so I've kayaked down the Yukon from source to mouth and skied to the North Pole, which gave me a healthy dose of nature and physical exercise, as well as plenty of time training and working hard with mates. I'm not for one minute suggesting that you take on such a serious level of risk, or make such a big time commitment, when picking your requirements for a proactive mission, but there are two key elements that should be incorporated for maximum results:

- The challenge needs to feel both scary and inspirational at the same time. Think: a test that requires you to overcome a fear, such as a dislike of heights or public speaking.
- The task should include some element of nature because periods of time spent outdoors can have a hugely positive impact on our physical and mental well-being. Either experience the environment 1) directly, through the challenge itself, or 2) indirectly, as a restorative break from whatever it is you're doing.

As for everything else, that's entirely up to you.

TACTICAL BRIEFING: PICK YOUR TARGET

There are all sorts of ways in which you can select your next mission. It might be that you've already got a clear sense of your objectives. Maybe there's a wide range of ideas, in which case stick the list to a wall and lob a dart at it, or go *The Dice Man** route and randomize your choice. If you want a more considered approach – one that will guarantee a more fulfilling experience – then leaning into the Japanese concept of *ikigai* might shine a light on to your interests, skills and drives, and help to identify an inspirational challenge; feeling highly motivated is the best way of lasting the course when the going gets rough – which, if you're pushing your boundaries, it most definitely will.

Ikigai means 'a reason to live', and comprises four elements: passion (something you love doing), profession (your talents), vocation (a skill you can be paid for) and mission (a cause that helps others). A person will usually experience a greater sense of purpose when overlapping these personal factors, as I discovered while recovering from PTSD following my departure from the military. At the time, I was lost, unable to function in a 'normal' job I hated, with no real sense of purpose or love for what I was doing. In the end, my application of *ikigai* was accidental; I had no idea it even existed, but through therapy I discovered its four elements, which helped me to find a new life that was close to my heart:

- **Passion: I challenged myself in harsh, outdoor environments.**
- **Profession: I worked myself physically.**
- **Vocation: I made money by sharing my experiences on television.**
- **Mission: I talked openly about my psychological struggles and recovery.**

My *ikigai:* To help people struggling with mental health issues.

* The Dice Man *is a novel written by Luke Rhinehart, in which the main character, a psychiatrist, makes all his decisions based on the roll of a dice.*

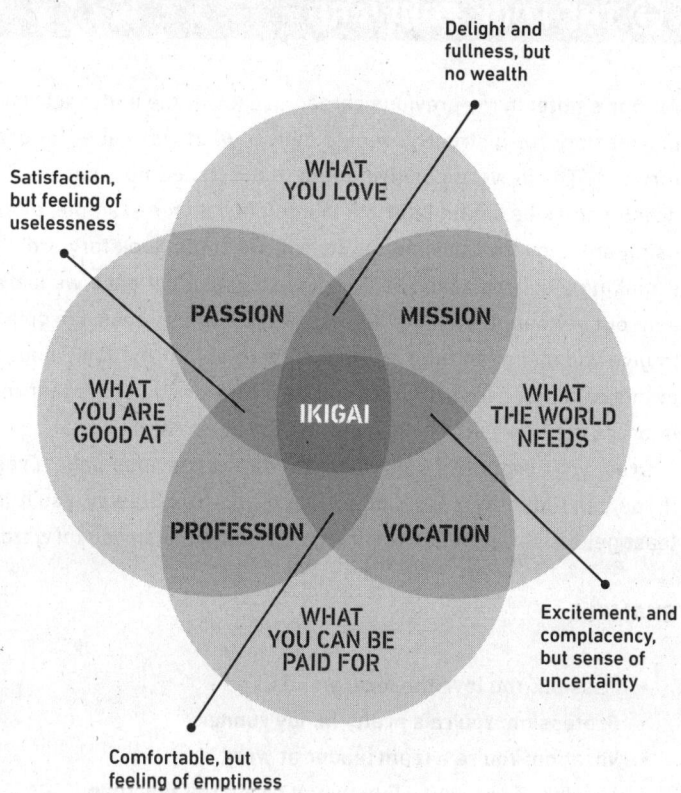

So, if you're struggling to imagine your next mission, take a look at the illustration above. Then consider all four elements of *ikigai*. Because, if you can get a handle on the things that excite you the most in life, you'll find the motivating factors for your next mission.

⊙ THE LOOK FORWARD

Author's note: In my previous career, usually at the end of a training session, our instructors would deliver what was called a 'look forward'. These were positive notes that detailed how our newly developed skills would later come into play. So for example, after using an innovative piece of optics kit, we could 'look forward' to it making our lives easier in the theatre of conflict once we were sent out on tour. At the end of every chapter in this book, I'm going to give you a similar, future-facing snippet of information. Though in this case, your look forward will be a task or challenge that reinforces the message I've been trying to get across.

Draw your *ikigai* using the diagram on the previous page. Even if you can't identify a mission for yourself straightaway, you'll at least get a clearer idea of the things that might push you forward.

EXAMPLE
....

- **Passion:** You love the local woods.
- **Profession:** You're a pretty handy runner.
- **Vocation:** You're a team leader at work.
- **Mission:** To organize the annual 5K or 10K woodland race in the area.

Your *ikigai:* To boost the community by bringing people together through a shared love of exercise and the local environment.

CHAPTER 2
THE FEAR FACTOR

Fear is your friend, and tackling that reality, though daunting, is often an incredibly positive experience. I've certainly had to endure episodes of terror throughout my life, but in doing so I've come to understand the benefits. When diving underwater in the pitch black, when parachuting away from a plane, when fast-roping from a helicopter on to a heavily armed drug boat: if ever I've felt frightened in those situations, it's reminded me, weirdly, that I'm still alive, especially if my body was close to breaking point. Somehow, I always managed to work through the stress.

'Quit moaning,' I'd say, 'and get on with it.'

Having pushed past the fear and achieved my targets, I then became emboldened. My confidence and sense of well-being soared. *I wanted to feel the fear again.*

I can't stress this enough: staring down the things that frighten you the most is a valuable experience because you'll become a much tougher prospect as a result. Examples might include flying, confrontation with others, open water, being separated from home and family, or confined spaces. Having identified one or two issues, give yourself a challenge so that the facing of a fear becomes inevitable. This will ensure that an emotional uplift takes place once the task has been executed. (A quick side note: in a reactive mission, there's a good chance you'll be scared at some point anyway. Know that growth will happen as a consequence of simply taking a series of positive steps, which I'll detail in the Tactical Briefing.)

Stuck for inspiration? Consider the following jumping-off points:

- **You experience social anxiety in a group setting: take up acting or a night class in order to meet people and push your boundaries with strangers.**
- **In confrontational flashpoints you lack authority: take up boxing or martial arts (for the confidence it brings, not the headshots).**
- **Being alone gives you the creeps: travel solo to an unfamiliar city or country.**

If you can overcome a fear during a mission, the transformational results that follow will be noticeable. I've seen people push beyond their insecurities so they could achieve amazing things. A couple of years ago I invited the comedian Rob Delaney to North Wales for the television show *Foxy's Fearless 48 Hours*, in which I took celebrities on unsettling adventures. By his own admission, Rob was emotionally stagnating, which was understandable because he'd experienced tragedy when his two-year-old son died from a brain tumour in 2018. Alcoholism had been a problem, too. In 2002, he'd nearly killed himself, having blacked out behind the wheel of his car and crashed into a building. Surrounded by doctors and police officers in a hospital ward, Rob then asked if anyone else had been hurt. He had no real idea of what had happened. Luckily, he'd been the only casualty.

OK, there is no shadow of a doubt here, thought Rob. *My drinking, which I've known for some years is dangerous to me . . . Now I know other people are in danger, I'm not going to do that.*

It was clear Rob was stuck in a bad place following the death of his son and, by his own account, he hadn't taken any risks in his life since his twenties. To help him re-boot, I wanted Rob to face his fear of heights, first by having him 'tombstone' into a water-filled quarry from a ledge positioned thirty feet up. His next tests were to crawl across a high-wire above a ninety-metre drop and then freefall from a 150-foot-high viaduct. Having nailed all three challenges, Rob emerged from the mission with a new perspective on life.

'These last couple of days were a big deal,' he said afterwards. 'I think they've helped me to process a lot of stuff, helped me organize some feelings and beliefs about life. But they've also helped me reorder my priorities in a way that I'll really work to have stick with me.'

The same can happen for you, too.

TACTICAL BRIEFING: STEP TO THE EDGE . . . SLOWLY

Don't wreck your head by jumping straight in at the deep end. Instead, if you're actively facing a fear (I repeat: *you should be*), it's my recommendation that you try a form of exposure therapy, a therapeutic process that first emerged in England during the 1950s in which a phobia is managed step-by-step and in small increments. A good case study for this would be the person who hates crowds. Step One would be for them to visit a crowded supermarket, followed by a rush-hour bus journey for Step Two. At first they'll feel a surge of panic, but having settled into an emotionally chaotic environment they should be able to calm themselves quite comfortably. A good location for Step Three would be a lower-league football match or a comedy show. Step Four might require them to spend the day at a busy music festival. The idea is that their anxiety will diminish with time and repeated exposure, as shown in the chart overleaf.

This process was perfectly illustrated when I travelled to Australia a couple of years ago to record *SAS: Who Dares Wins*. Having been placed into hotel quarantine for two weeks, I found

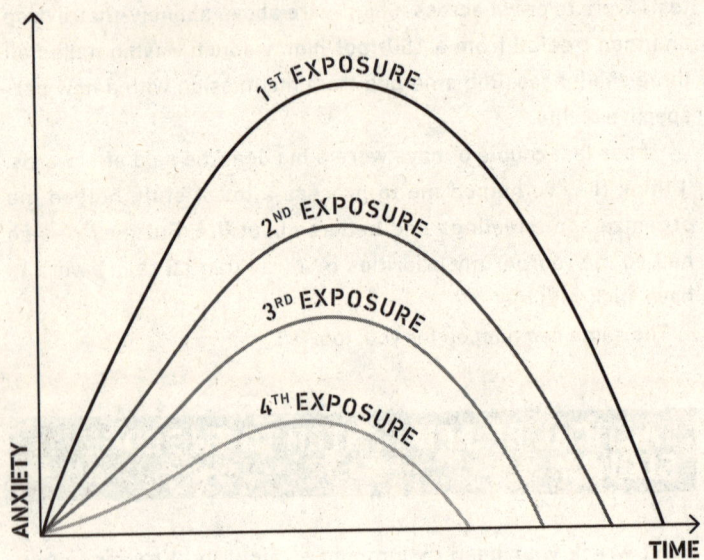

myself stuck on the eighteenth floor and, like Rob Delaney, I'm not great with heights. But knowing I would have to abseil, climb and perform a high-wire crossing over a ravine during filming, I decided to work through some exposure therapy of my own. Outside my room was a balcony with a glass front that separated me from a horrific drop to the street below. Rather than avoiding it, I stood at the edge every day and stared down at the ant-like crowds below for a set period of time, noting the reduced levels of anxiety as I did so. When it came to working at height during production, I felt much calmer than I would have done ordinarily.

⊖ THE LOOK FORWARD

List your fears, then write down four progressive stages of exposure therapy for each one.

EXAMPLE

SWIMMING IN OPEN WATER FREAKS YOU OUT.

- **Step One:** Spend some time in a tidal pool.
- **Step Two:** Go paddle boarding, or take a boating trip at the ocean.
- **Step Three:** Take a wild-swimming lesson.
- **Step Four:** Join a coastal swimming group, or book a snorkelling trip on holiday.

CHAPTER 3
INTO THE WILD

Testing myself in challenging environments has been a big part of my life. For much of my military career, I crawled around in the mud and dirt. I was tossed about by rolling seas, and suffered the heat and suffocation of intimidating desert landscapes. Later, while figuring out my life away from war, I dived on shipwrecks, protected rhinos from poachers in the Barberton Makhonjwa Mountains in South Africa and rowed across the Atlantic Ocean. But despite the physical hardships of these expeditions, I came to understand that a deep connection with nature is often beneficial, for three reasons:

- The sensation of being overawed by the environment was always incredible, even when it was threatening to kill me.
- There was no compromising with the wild, and I loved it: it's impossible to talk your way out of a hurricane or a snowstorm, and if you ever see a grizzly bear approaching, run – *sharpish*. Taking on the natural world and coming away relatively unscathed always gave me a sense of achievement.
- Being outdoors was good for my mental health. I felt calm, less worried about the stresses in my life and able to focus on what was truly important.

One example of how challenging myself in nature delivered all three of these uplifts took place in 2020, when the world was feeling fed up at what seemed like a never-ending succession of pandemic-related restrictions. Rather than slobbing about on the sofa, I decided to flick my switches by travelling to the nearby countryside in a series of 'explore local' challenges with my former Royal Marines teammate Aldo Kane. Our aims were to operate outdoors in a series of physical challenges while living on a shoestring budget. We also wanted to escape our comfort zones and inspire anyone following us on social media to do the same. This was done by first executing a hairy, three-pitch climb across a series of sea cliffs. We followed that up by scaling trees, setting hammocks and sleeping in the woods (after a few tins of cider). Finally the pair of us conducted a thirteen-metre free dive into a flooded quarry, where we explored a sunken aircraft. It was an epic trip – at times I felt calmed, overawed and exhilarated by surviving in the wild conditions.

Finding enjoyment in challenges of this kind isn't unique to me or Aldo. It's not a trait that can be traced back to my childhood, nor is it part of some exclusive genetic blueprint found only in the military or expedition elite. The truth is that every single one of us can reap the rewards of working in an untamed environment, because we've all been designed to thrive and survive in nature, whether we believe it's possible or not. As *Celebrity SAS: Who Dares Wins* has shown me, a pampered person can grow in all sorts of ways when separated from the comfort and artificiality of a centrally heated building – though it may not feel that way for them at first. Not when they're up to their waist in a freezing lake or sweating their bollocks off during a physical thrashing.

That same reaction can happen to all of us, and it can take place at the extreme end of the scale, like during a high-altitude ultra-marathon, or in more benign circumstances, such as a swim in a river or a lake. Just the simple concept of 'forest bathing' (a fancy phrase to describe a walk in the woods) has been proven to help with the management of mental health issues such as depression, anxiety, confusion and anger (as revealed in a 2007 study, *Psychological Effects of Forest Environments on Healthy Adults,* co-authored by several researchers in Japan).

This conclusion isn't based solely on anecdotal evidence, either. Positive changes to a person's blood pressure are known to take place when walking in nature; the body's sympathetic nerve activity – which is thought to trigger our fight-or-flight response – is also known to decrease. It's unsurprising that in Canada doctors now prescribe free national-park passes for patients experiencing mental health problems. The process is known as ecotherapy.

I recommend you make it a priority to test yourself in the natural environment in some way. Of course, not all of us will have immediate access to National Trust woodlands or a series of rolling hills, but that's no real barrier to experiencing the outdoors. Even taking some time to walk around the local park can be helpful.

TACTICAL BRIEFING: MAXIMIZE YOUR ENVIRONMENT

When planning your next mission, try to involve nature in one of three ways: direct, indirect and abstract.

DIRECT

Make nature the challenge. Walk all ninety-six miles of the West Highland Way in Scotland, climb a mountain, or take your first wild-camping trip. It might be that you're planning to run or walk 100 miles in a month for charity, in which case yomp across your nearest fells or run through the woods, rather than pound the streets around your house or hammer a treadmill.

INDIRECT

If your challenge is work-related or based indoors, make sure a part of your daily routine takes place outdoors in the park or woods. Evidence suggests that our working memory, attention span and cognitive abilities improve after time spent in a natural environment.

ABSTRACT

If, for whatever reason, you're unable to reach the nearest beach, park or forest, pick up a meditation app and listen to the sound of crashing waves on a beach, or some other natural soundscape. These noises provide a soothing, non-threatening environment as you work or rest. Meanwhile, it's known that you can lower inflammation levels in the body by simply staring at nature and experiencing a sense of awe.

⊙ THE LOOK FORWARD

For the next week, take a twenty-minute daily walk at your nearest wood, beach or park (and leave your phone at home). Make a note of how you feel before, during and after each trip to gain an understanding of how your emotional state changes.

CHAPTER 4
PLAN THE HELL OUT OF IT

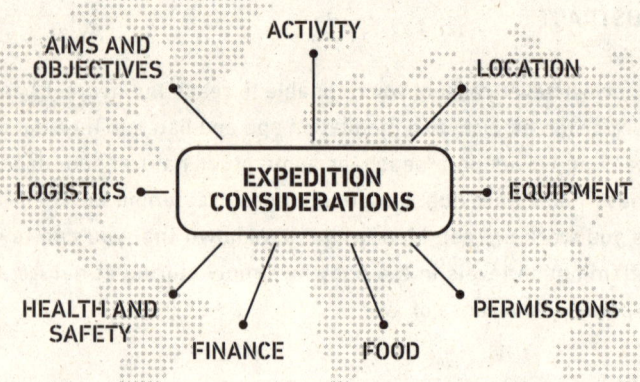

AIMS AND OBJECTIVES

ACTIVITY

LOCATION

LOGISTICS

EXPEDITION CONSIDERATIONS

EQUIPMENT

HEALTH AND SAFETY

FINANCE

FOOD

PERMISSIONS

The planning phase of any mission can sometimes feel like a challenge in and of itself – *the mission within a mission* – but there's usually an emotional benefit to be enjoyed afterwards: just the act of prepping an operation can deliver a huge boost to the individuals involved, and that's because planning and goal-setting causes the brain to release dopamine. Nicknamed the 'Dr Feelgood Chemical' (because it acts as the name suggests), this transmitter is responsible for keeping us attentive and motivated (as well as being responsible for our moods and memory) by linking positive feelings to certain behaviours. For example, the satisfaction we get when nailing tasks and ticking boxes as we approach an important deadline.

I know one of my favourite parts of any mission is the planning phase. I get a buzz from researching technical kit and listing the supplies needed to survive. I even like to visualize where I'm going, what I'll be doing and the type of challenges I might face. Am I odd? *Maybe.* But this love for planning was born in the military, where the units I served in carried a mega-boner for logistics. During my time in service, elite-level organization was one of the things that maintained a level of superiority over our enemy and, unsurprisingly, I've since carried the same attitude towards preparation and discipline into my missions outside of war – whether they're big or small, proactive or reactive. So far it's helped to keep me in one piece. It's for that reason that planning a mission to the nth degree will be a psychological benefit to you, too. (Even if you're not actually going on one, as I'll explain shortly.)

When it comes to mission-planning, however, it's no good me running through a set of random jobs with my head on fire. If I'm to operate effectively, my goals have to be mission-critical and structured. For that reason I've developed a list of ten fixed categories that have to be squared away if I'm to feel suitably prepared before an operation.

To help show you how this process works, I'm going to detail a potential mission in my calendar. The brief: in the coming year or so, I hope to kayak down the Mackenzie River in Canada. I'll be accompanied by my mate Sean Johnson, a seasoned explorer who I teamed up with during a two-man, unsupported journey down the length of the Yukon River in 2019 – all 1,980 miles of it. As we plan, I'll focus my attention on these ten key areas:

OBJECTIVES: WHY AM I DOING THIS?

To kayak down the Mackenzie River, a part of the world I really want to see, and to do so before climate change affects the ecosystem. Elsewhere, I'd like to put my skills to the test in an extreme environment, work outdoors with a mate and hopefully raise a chunk of money for charity.

ACTIVITY: WHAT WILL I BE DOING?

A lot of kayaking. This is bound to be a physical grind, so I'll have to figure out an appropriate training programme. The mission will be a reset for my head, too.

LOCATION: WHERE AM I GOING?

Well, an extremely long river in Canada. I'm going to be beasted by the rapids and dunked into the freezing water, over and over. Feeling cold, wet and hungry is going to be the norm. I'll also have to keep an eye out for the local bears.

EQUIPMENT: WHAT DO I NEED TO GET THE JOB DONE?

In addition to camping gear and some sturdy clothing, the most important piece of kit will be my kayak. As the mission approaches, Sean and I will discuss the canoes best suited to the Mackenzie; we'll research where to buy them and how to transport both to our starting point.

PERMISSIONS: IS THERE ANY PAPERWORK TO SORT?

I need a river permit and a tourist visa for my entry into Canada. Emergency insurance is vital, too.

FOOD: WHAT DO I NEED TO STAY PHYSICALLY AND MENTALLY STRONG?

In advance of the trip, I'll work out the best- and worst-case scenarios for the mission duration. Then I'll estimate the amount of supplies needed to survive the latter. Given there's a series of villages and outposts on the Mackenzie, we can resupply our stocks as we travel.

FINANCE: HOW AM I PAYING FOR THIS?

Bank balances will need to be assessed before committing to the mission (I don't want to ruin myself). Costs will include flights, visas and permits, food, equipment, accommodation and insurance, plus an emergency fund if things go south.

HEALTH AND SAFETY: WHAT HAPPENS IF WE GET STUCK, OR BADLY HURT?

One of us should carry a satellite phone in case we need to be lifted away at some point.

LOGISTICS: WHAT'S THE ROUTE FROM BEGINNING TO END?

In addition to plotting the course, it's vital I research the Mackenzie's most dangerous features and the other areas in which we might experience problems, such as rapids. It helps to create a clear picture of our route, including where to camp (and where not to).

THE END: WHAT HAPPENS NEXT?

After the mission is completed I'll decompress and analyse my experience in such a way that I can learn from it. Then I'll reset and go again.

TACTICAL BRIEFING: FORGET FOOLPROOF

No matter how much groundwork you've conducted in advance, the perfect mission plan doesn't exist. So while it's important to prep, it's also vital we give ourselves a little wriggle room should things go wrong, which they often do. For example, on the Yukon expedition, Sean and I decided to fly over all the food needed for an expedition of two months. We blew approximately two grand on rations, though carrying the lot for an entire journey felt like a ball-ache. Then one of us had the bright idea of shipping everything from our starting point at Whitehorse to Fort Yukon, a location further down the river.

Sadly, we were screwed upon our arrival at Whitehorse: 'There hasn't been a post office in Fort Yukon for about ten years,' said a postal worker in the town, looking down at our supplies.

This was a monumental cock-up on our part. We'd forgotten to check these particular logistics in advance, but there was no way the situation was going to derail us. Instead, we formulated a new plan and moved forward with a positive mindset. Step One was to pack a small amount of food in the kayaks. Step Two was to give the rest of our scran to a local family who were taking their kids away on a camping trip. Step Three was to replenish our supplies at local stores as we progressed along the Yukon. Neither of us felt deflated. Sean and I had long understood that no plan was 100 per cent bombproof, so there was little point in us expecting perfection. That was a sure-fire route to disappointment; whereas rolling with the punches, while bringing a positive mindset, was the fastest line to success.

→ THE LOOK FORWARD

Whatever your mission or objective, draw up the checklist and fill in all ten criteria. It might be that you're about to learn a new language, or you're looking for a new house: the task ahead really doesn't matter; the important thing is to build a coherent roadmap by identifying the targets you'll need to hit in order to be ready. If there's no immediate challenge on the horizon, dream up an exciting expedition you hope to take one day. The process should encourage you to visualize it, and will deliver a healthy shot of dopamine.

CHAPTER 5
MISSION-SPECIFIC TRAINING

Before every military tour there was usually a period of mission-specific training, where I would be readied for any specialized or unusual situations that might arise. For example, if we were heading into a region where civil unrest was expected, the lads would run through a riot-training course. Before operations, if gathered intelligence had developed a layout of the compound we were attacking, our group would mark its perimeters on the ground – with tyres and tape – and literally walk through the assault. As we did so, various instructions would be dished out by senior command, such as how best to deal with the hostiles in a certain position, or where to take cover in case of an emergency.

No detail was left to chance. We swotted up on our skills and we refreshed our knowledge. We did our medical and weapons training, and worked on our mobility. We even practised for worst-case scenarios with recovery drills. If a vehicle became bogged down in the terrain, everyone on the ground knew exactly what to do in order to get it moving again. In much the same way, Sean and I had deliberately capsized our kayaks in the run-up to the Yukon trip, so we would know how to react in the event of an accident.

This laser-focused approach is vital for any mission to succeed. I know, because I've used it over and over again. In 2016, when I rowed across the Atlantic with Team Essence – a five-man crew comprising Mathew Bennet, Ross Johnson and Oliver Bailey, plus Aldo Kane and myself – in what was a world-record-setting, unsupported epic over fifty days, I did as much mission-specific training as I could in advance. I worked for hours on a stationary rower to ensure my body was strong, and I lubed-up my joints with omega-3. My head was readied by constantly visualizing the physical pain to come. During a holiday, I sat on the beach and imagined the overwhelming sense of isolation that would hit me in the middle of a vast body of water. Between myself and the other lads, Team Essence figured out the workings of the vessel's comms and navigation equipment, and how to fix the boat if it broke, in all manner of ways. (I made a point of taking a shitload of string, gaffer tape and wire with me because these always came in handy when repairing rudders and oars.)

Really this was no different from a military mission, where we practised for every grim eventuality during the build-up. That way, when one of them happened for real, nobody flapped or lost heart, because through mission-specific training we had learned how to navigate disaster.

TACTICAL BRIEFING: ANALYSE YOUR CHALLENGE – WHAT IS IT THAT MAKES YOUR MISSION UNIQUE?

Every situation can be prepared for. It could be that you're about to take on a series of educational assessments, in which case, replicate the pressures associated with an exam room. When the tests come around for real, you'll feel comfortable in what might be a very uncomfortable setting. Or maybe you're meeting an important business client for the very first time. If so, practise making a confident impression with your appearance and body language, and have a mental checklist of the points you'd like to get across. (You can do all of this by simply practising in front of a mirror.)

An interesting example of this technique was used by the

Arsenal manager Mikel Arteta, while readying his young side for an away trip at Liverpool during the 2021/22 Premier League campaign. Liverpool famously play at Anfield, which is regarded by most players as an intimidating cauldron – their fans are usually up for it. To prepare his squad for the experience, Arteta forced them to train while a set of speakers positioned around the pitch played Liverpool's famous anthem 'You'll Never Walk Alone'. While the concept might have been flawed practically – there's really no way of fully creating the hostile atmosphere of a rammed football stadium, and Arsenal were beaten soundly in the end – Arteta's aims were solid. His hope was to steady his side for what would be an emotionally brutal experience by taking an interesting approach to mission-specific training. His team were likely better prepared as a result.

You can do the same. Simply identify your mission's unique challenges and then prepare accordingly. It might not prove to be the defining factor between success and failure, but it will help you to function effectively should things go belly-up.

⊕ THE LOOK FORWARD

Assess your mission and figure out a suitable training plan. If you're going on a road cycling challenge, ride the course in advance – you'll soon discover any flaws in your race strategy. Or if you're starting a new job in a new city, take the commute a few days earlier, at the height of rush hour, so you can avoid any pitfalls and arrive on time for your first day.

CHAPTER 6
TRAIN TO FAIL

Resilience isn't built in moments of victory – it grows in failure. Which is why, during my military training, I was forever being pushed into situations where it seemed as if things were falling apart in a big way. During exercises, our instructors – or umpires – often lobbed a curveball at us, usually when we were at our lowest ebb, and I hated it. The most common trick was for them to point at a couple of operators, in the middle of an exercise, and shout, 'Right! You and you: you're seriously injured. The rest of you: what are you going to do about it?' It would then be down to the group to formulate an extraction plan. But during those moments of intense pain, as I lugged a teammate around a boggy field in the freezing cold, I often learned the most about myself. There was always a realization about my capabilities or resilience. *Knowledge dispelled fear*. And when that same incident happened for real, when I was helping to drag a seriously injured operator away from a gunfight, my brain and body knew exactly what to expect and I thrived.

One time, I was involved in an exercise on Salisbury Plain. As we approached our collection point, two Chinook helicopters landed on the top of a knoll. Everyone was loading on to the bird, when suddenly one of our instructors shouted to me and another operator.

'You two: you've been cut off from the rest of the team. You're going to miss those choppers and you're going into Escape and Evasion.'

I sighed. That would require us to go on the run and avoid detection for around forty-eight hours.

'Are you joking? I'm here at the helicopter—'

The umpire shook his head. 'Nope. You've missed it. And you need to get out of here because you're about to get rolled up by the enemy.'

For a split second, my heart sank. I should have been flying back to the base for a kip and a gallon of hot tea. Instead, I was to be spending the next forty-eight hours on Salisbury Plain, sleeping in the bushes and moving under the cover of darkness in the tipping rain. In the end it became a massive learning lesson, and one I was pleased to have experienced, mainly because it delivered a kick up the arse that showed me I had to be switched on at all times. The helicopters had arrived before we had, when we should have been waiting for *them*. (On a mission it's important to never leave a helicopter waiting, where they might be exposed to enemy attack.) During those two days in the outdoors, being cold, wet and knackered, *and surviving*, showed me that if ever I was split up from my team for real, I had it in me to make it home.

The beauty of training to fail – for any mission – is that it becomes much easier to spot any potential screw-ups ahead of time, and in all manner of situations. Recently I was invited on to a podcast hosted by a mate of mine. He had just bought the latest studio recording kit – it was fancy, with flashing lights all over the place and a bank of dials and knobs. But this was his first outing with the equipment and very little of it had been battle-tested. *He hadn't trained to fail.* And after interviewing me for about an hour, the host suddenly put his hand up.

'Mate, I didn't press record.'

'Fuck off. You're not serious.'

'I am,' he said. 'We've got to do it again.'

'No way. I've got to make a three-hour drive home. I haven't got the time . . .'

By not putting his kit through a real-time interview situation and stress-testing his rig with a simulated failure, my mate hadn't noticed his set-up wasn't working properly. Had he trained to fail, there's a good chance he'd have realized at an early stage that things weren't right and saved us both a lot of trouble and time.

Overall, throwing one or two curveballs at your operational procedures can help to bombproof missions in a few ways, so remember the following pointers about working through moments of failure:

- At your lowest ebb, you'll learn a lot about yourself and how you operate.
- In a team setting, you'll discover who can be relied upon in moments of high stress, and who can't. (And that person might be you.)
- Knowledge brings strength: disaster can highlight weaknesses you might not have realized were there, allowing you to improve upon them.
- In the aftermath of a screw-up, failure will seem less frightening and will show you that in times of trouble, there's usually a way out.

You only come to these understandings through experience – so bring it on.

TACTICAL BRIEFING: THE WORST COURSE OF ACTION

Before any mission, the senior command often presented operators with two possible outcomes: the most likely course of action, and the worst. The most likely course of action was designed to reassure the blokes involved that we were the dominant force and far superior to the hostiles we were facing. We had the best training, the best weaponry and the best technology. This talk was done subtly. It wasn't as if we were running around the briefing room, or high-fiving one another, and anyone who might have been experiencing an expanding ego was quickly brought down to earth by a reminder of the worst course of action – specifically, what could go wrong and what to do in the event of a monumental balls-up.

This follow-up statement had an equally important impact. It created a ripple of nervousness throughout the group and reminded everyone involved to remain on high alert. But just as the most likely course of action instilled the right amount of confidence within the group, so the worst course of action created the right amount of anxiety. Everyone became much sharper as a result and any complacency was killed. This was most important whenever a mission went south. I remember being pinned down by gunfire for extended periods of time, and watching as my air support disappeared for fuel. But those moments of high stress never came as too much of a shock, because they were curveballs I'd been prepared for. As a result, when everything turned to shit, I knew exactly how to cope.

When heading into any mission, ask yourself two questions:

- **What's the likeliest course of action?**
- **And what's the worst?**

Steadying yourself for both will help you to avoid any nasty surprises.

⊕ THE LOOK FORWARD

As you prepare, stress-test your mission with a curveball situation. Then assess your reactions.

EXAMPLES

- Set a self-imposed and very tight false deadline for a work project. *How do you cope under pressure?*
- Train without the support of a vital piece of kit or equipment. *How will you adapt?*
- Imagine that you've had a system failure: prepare for someone going sick at work by familiarizing yourself with some of their most valuable tasks and responsibilities. *How will you operate without them?*

CHAPTER 7
PRE-
PERFORMANCE
ROUTINE

On the eve of any major mission it's important we ready ourselves with a pre-performance routine – a series of actions that, if applied properly, can ensure we're in the best possible state of mind to operate effectively. During my time in elite service, these procedures comprised:

- A full brief of what was expected, including the resources at hand and the capabilities of our enemy.
- An understanding of the skills required to succeed.
- A period of training to learn or practise those skills (if we didn't have them already).
- The preparation of kit, intelligence, briefing details, etc. This usually took place the day before.
- Time to rest so the group could hit peak performance at exactly the right moment.

By following the same processes, over and over, we were able to effectively understand what needed to be done and how to do it, all while ensuring we were in the best position to complete our tasks effectively.

Everything in the military was geared towards the concept of pre-performance routines. Nobody rocked up to a gunfight with zero preparation for what was to come. Even before I'd completed my first day of Basic Training with the Royal Marines, I was steadied with induction courses and briefings. I even read books and magazines that told me of the painful realities of life as a serving commando. On day one of Basic Training, I was under no illusions as to what was waiting for me.

This concept was ramped up once I'd joined the military elite, where pre-performance routines were mapped out in incredibly high detail. Before every job, the group as a whole was given the details of the mission, which included an intelligence briefing and operational outline. All the t's were crossed and the i's were dotted, right down to the radio frequencies we would be talking on. Once that information was delivered, the group would split into smaller units, with each one being given a clear set of instructions for their role in the larger mission. Everyone knew explicitly what they had to do, how they were supposed to do it, and the type of kit and weaponry they would be required to bring. Provided there was enough time on the clock, the operators involved would run through a rehearsal phase.

Finally we took care of our personal admin. In the days building up to the big event, it was on the individual to rest well, eat the right foods and drink enough water, because missions could go tits-up and an operator might be expected to live on his wits for days on end (though it was important not to consume too much. I was always paranoid about overhydrating, because it was no good running on to the helicopter and realizing you needed to go for a piss, or worse.) However, if all of those pre-performance routines had been completed – and nobody soiled themselves – most jobs tended to run smoothly.

Well, as smoothly as could be expected in a war zone.

TACTICAL BRIEFING: DESIGN YOUR PRE-PERFORMANCE ROUTINE

These same processes can be applied to any type of mission. For example, I hate public speaking. I feel nervous and my palms get sweaty, which is a problem because I have to do a lot of corporate appearances and speaking gigs. During the build-up to my first-ever theatre tour one Christmas, I remember receiving the final draft of the scripts we'd been working on. While everyone around me was having a good time, getting stuck into the festive spirit, I was reading line after line of dialogue and going into a flat spin.

Oh, fuck, I said to myself. *I'm never going to be able to remember all of this.*

I thought about the actors in plays and musicals, and wondered how the hell they were able to remember all that word salad. I was petrified. I convinced myself that people who had it in them to stand on-stage and recite a twenty-page monologue were gifted and that it would be beyond me. Then I remembered I'd felt that way about the military's elite groups when I first signed up with the Royal Marines.

They were special.

No way could I do what they did.

But I had been able to put those doubts to bed with a basic pre-performance routine, so there was no reason I couldn't do the same with my scripts and a looming tour of daunting venues, especially as my skill sets had been upgraded in elite service.

In the end, I worked through an effective process in much the same way the lads and I had done for missions. This took on the five key phases:

PHASE ONE: A FULL BRIEF

My hope was to give the audience an insight into my career and the battles I experienced with mental health, with some funny stories thrown in.

PHASE TWO: WHAT SKILLS WERE REQUIRED?

I worked out how long I needed to chat for, which was two, one-hour-long chunks (these were separated by an interval, so the audience could pop off for a beer). I had to speak clearly, with no ums and ahs, and keep the audience engaged. Most of all, I had to be funny. No pressure, then.

PHASE THREE: A PERIOD OF TRAINING

The bloke who had helped with my scripts was an actor and voice artist. As well as giving me one or two pointers on delivery, he also helped to prepare me for the shows with some self-calming techniques, though I wasn't convinced at first.

'You need to get big before a performance,' he said. 'Stand in front of a mirror, imagine yourself as Superman or Batman, and strike a pose.'

Fuck off, mate.

'Seriously, it helps.'

Reluctantly, I gave it a go and, bloody hell, it worked. I stood up tall like a DC Comics superhero and sucked in a deep breath. All of a sudden, I felt much lighter. I was relaxed. The technique helped to dissipate a lot of the fear I'd been experiencing.

PHASE FOUR: A PERIOD OF PREPARATION

Even though I had some prompts at the front of the stage – in case I fluffed any of my lines, or stiffed – I was determined to learn the script off by heart. After all, it was my story, not someone else's. I wanted it to feel authentic, so I spent weeks reciting large chunks of text, over and over, until I'd memorized the lot. It gave me more confidence, which helped to improve my delivery.

PHASE FIVE: RESTING FOR PEAK PERFORMANCE

Getting on-stage and telling my story was one of the scariest things I've ever done, so to make sure I was in the right frame of mind to deliver a good show every night, I stuck to my regular training routine as I travelled up and down the country. I even cut back on the booze to reduce my anxiety levels.

Once put in motion, this pre-performance routine helped me to deliver consistently on a nightly basis. I'm sure there were one or two dud nights, but I felt pretty chuffed overall and this helped me to create a positive feedback loop. Backed by a series of actions that were pushing me to succeed, I developed new skills. These new skills created an increased level of competence, which, in turn, boosted my confidence levels, to the point where I'd happily do another tour without too much stress – although a little nervousness can be considered a good thing: the butterflies ensure we remain switched on.

⊕ THE LOOK FORWARD

Create a pre-performance routine for your forthcoming mission. Write down the challenge and the skills required to succeed. Then work out how best to learn and master those skills. As the mission approaches do a dry run if possible and structure a window of time in which you can ready your equipment, double-check the logistics of whatever it is you want to do, and deal with any last-minute admin. Finally, work out what you'll need to do in order to feel physically and mentally primed for the test ahead.

CHAPTER 8
CREATE YOUR OPERATIONAL RITUALS

When I walked around the base on military tours I'd sometimes see a teammate standing in front of the mirror, raising their weapon from a resting position, over and over and over. Likewise, it wasn't uncommon to spot lads creeping around corners, or stacking up outside a door as if they were about to kick it in. To an outsider, these scenes would have resembled a bunch of kids playing war, except the differences couldn't have been any starker: in real-life conflicts, the split-second between firing off a round, or not, or approaching a door effectively, was the difference between life and death. By practising those skills, even in front of a mirror, an individual was improving their muscle memory by the tiniest of percentages. It ensured their technique remained on point when it really mattered.

It's not just in combat that these actions come into play. Watch a professional golfer before he or she takes their shot. Every time, without fail, they'll stand behind the ball and assess the lie, wind, target ahead and the various obstacles in play, such as a bunker or tree. This is followed by a few seconds of visualization, where the perfect shot is imagined. Finally, following a few practice swings, the player settles over their ball with a deep breath, and following a mental or physical trigger point, they'll start their swing. It's the same for penalty takers in football or basketball players preparing to take a free throw. In moments of high pressure, the elite player will call upon an operational routine so they can deliver effectively.

To some fans, these processes might look like habits or even superstitions (and of course, operators and athletes often lean upon these too). But in reality, they're a short series of drills designed to reduce stress, silence negative thoughts and set up an individual for success by reinforcing the skills and techniques that they've honed over years of training. The same thing happens in other industries too:

- In the hour before signing an important deal, the CEO of a company might make a point of taking a final look at the contract on offer, run their eye over the market and remind themselves of the benefits of their latest move.
- To prepare for walking on-stage, some rock bands (Metallica being one) get together in a jam room to practise a few songs. The idea is to find a groove for showtime.
- Before conducting an interview, a journalist or podcast host will double-check the questions they want to ask and remind themselves of their most recent well-received feature or show.

While I was in the military, performing rituals of this kind was known as a pre-skill routine. Generally it required three steps:

A POSITIVE PSYCHOLOGICAL STRATEGY

On the eve of a job, I imagined the positive emotions I would feel at the end, with everything having gone to plan. When I'm working today, I carry this same feeling with me. If ever I get nervous about a corporate talk, TV show or media interview, I imagine how I'll feel in the green room with everything having gone well. That always settles me down. For you, a positive psychological strategy might involve imagining the rewarding meal, pint or holiday at the end of a successful challenge.

POSITIVE INNER DIALOGUE

No matter where I was scrapping, I reminded myself of the work I'd completed to get there and how it would help me to succeed again: I'd completed my Arctic training; I'd operated in the jungle, desert, mountains and all sorts of urban environments; I'd been able to function during moments of pain, fatigue, hunger and extreme stress.

'You've thrived in the worst places on earth,' I told myself. 'You can do it again.'

If you're feeling nervous about some aspect of the mission, recall an incident in which a moment of mental, emotional or physical pressure was overcome. You can do it again. *It's in you to repeat that success.*

A SEQUENCE OF BEHAVIOURS OR ACTIONS

This is a series of clearly defined movements and each one is designed to place a person into the right state of mind so they can execute effectively. In sport, one example of this would be the routine used by a tennis player as they prepare to serve the ball. In this scenario, the athlete might position their feet a certain way, take a series of breaths or bounce the ball a specific number of times. Remember: the sequence of events is supposed to be incredibly personal, and in order to ensure consistency the routine has to remain the same for every action. In parachute training, I practised an identical sequence of drills and movements before every jump. For you, this could mean running through a series of small actions before every meeting, exam, run, presentation, workout, deal, transaction or job interview. A consistent sequence will ensure a consistent performance.

TACTICAL BRIEFING: UNDERSTANDING THE STRESS CURVE

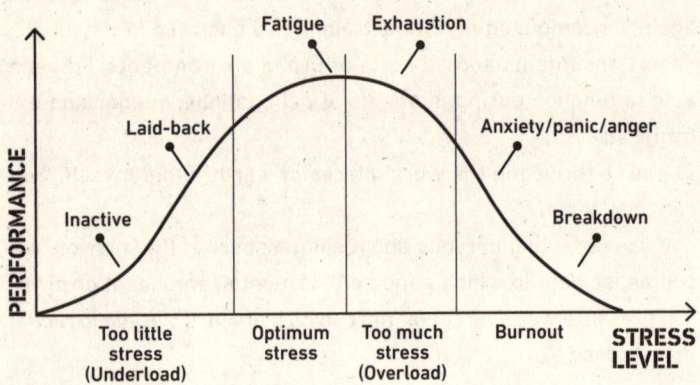

A little stress can help us to perform when it comes to executing a mission, task or skill, but the amount we experience is pivotal. Too much, and a person might overload emotionally or physically. Too little and there's a chance they'll become so relaxed that they're unable to perform at their peak. The sweet spot is found somewhere in the middle, as displayed in the 'Stress Curve' chart above by American behavioural investigator Vanessa Van Edwards.

'We perform at our best when we feel excited or aroused,' says Van Edwards on her website *Science of People*, 'but too much stress and we get exhausted or burnt-out.'

The key to avoiding burnout is to gain an understanding of the things that cause you to become overly stressed. If you've chosen to take on a challenge that requires you to face up to a fear, or deal with pressure, that could prove problematic. But don't worry: in those situations, simply tailor your pre-skill routine so that it allays those fears. So, for example, if you're about to compete in a sporting event, or perform in front of a large crowd for the very first time, reframe your fears as excitement. In his 2017 book *Psyched Up*, Daniel McGinn (a *Harvard Business Review* editor) explains how two groups of people were prepared for a karaoke-based video game in different ways. One group was told to shout, 'I'm so excited!' before their song. The other was instructed to yell, 'I'm so anxious!' The group boosted by positivity scored significantly higher in the game's performance-related rankings.

Interestingly, this reframing technique can also work for someone operating in the 'Underload' position on the Stress Curve. When we enter into a task we've performed a million times, it's easy to switch off and become complacent.

For example, stats show that 33 per cent of car crashes happen within a mile of the driver's home for this very reason. In which case, a pre-skill routine might involve:

- Visualizing a time when you felt nervous about driving, such as your first motorway experience (but where you came through successfully).
- A playlist of tunes that will help you to concentrate as you drive.
- Recalling your manoeuvres as you were taught them, like a learner.

This process might sound silly, but what's more embarrassing – checking your mirrors and signalling as you pull into the drive, or dinging a neighbour's car because you weren't paying attention?

⊕ THE LOOK FORWARD

Take some time to draw up a pre-skill ritual for the important tasks in your mission. These should include:

- **A psychological strategy to help you focus.**
- **A positive inner dialogue to boost your confidence, reduce nerves and get yourself sparking.**
- **A consistent series of actions that encourage you to perform to the best of your ability.**

CHAPTER 9
BE A SUCCESS IN YOUR HEAD

When conducting missions, visualization has become one of the most powerful tools in an elite soldier's psychological rig, though this was never explained explicitly to me when I was serving – I don't remember us ever being taught its importance. But these days the attitude towards mental preparation seems to be very different. Currently, personnel across the British Armed Forces are being taught the benefits of 'seeing' their missions in advance, whether they're fresh-faced recruits or Tier One operators, and there's a widely held belief that mentally performing a dry run of the challenge ahead can increase an individual's chances of success.

There's plenty of science to back up the theory. Whether we're performing for real or imagining the event from the comfort of our armchairs, neuroscientists have discovered that our brains will act in pretty much the same way.

In layman's terms the process works like this:

1) When visualizing a task or action we 'order' our brain to behave as if it were executing a task for real. For me, that task might be abseiling down a cliff; for you, it could be delivering a presentation, performing surgery or conducting an orchestra.

2) Our brain is full of neurons. These nerve cells chat to one another and create new pathways, which

then construct learned behaviours, whether we're
visualizing or performing.

3) These learned behaviours – muscle memory; an
emotional reaction to certain events or stimuli – kick
in when the event happens for real.

4) Our performances can improve as a result. We deliver
the presentation as we imagined. The techniques
used in surgery run smoothly, as we visualized. The
orchestra responds to our commands as our mental
rehearsal told us it would.

It's no surprise that visualization has long been used as a training tool for elite sports stars as they prepare for important matches or events. The Olympic swimming champion Michael Phelps is said to have mentally rerun his races in detail as he fell asleep, replaying them again during training sessions to intensify his motivation. Famously, the Russian chess prodigy Natan Sharansky played more than 1,000 matches in his head during a nine-year stint in a prison after he was accused of spying for the US during the Cold War. As he stared into space, the guards sometimes asked him what he was doing.

'Don't disturb me!' shouted Sharansky. 'I'm playing chess.'

After he was eventually freed, Sharansky went on to defeat the then world champ, Garry Kasparov.

I know from personal experience that visualization can be a massive resource in the build-up to any mission or challenge. Before raids, as I prepped my kit, or rested, I also readied my mind. I pictured myself moving through the enemy compound, clearing rooms and covering my teammates. I even pictured the more technical aspects of the work, such as the swim towards target. Importantly, I envisaged everything running smoothly: my weapon was always reloaded in double-quick time and I felt strong whenever I saw myself sprinting with a heavy bergen on my back.

Meanwhile, as I prepared for the more unpleasant aspects of the work, I also considered some of the emotions I might feel. Before every mission I told myself that I was stepping into a dangerous environment where there was a chance I might experience something horrendous, like the death of a mate. Thinking in that way prevented me from spinning out when something bad *did* happen, but it was important not to dwell on the negatives for too long – they could potentially overwhelm me if I did. That's why, whenever I stepped into a mission, I made sure to carry a positive mindset because it massively improved my chances of success. Getting fixated on the scarier stuff did exactly the opposite.

TACTICAL BRIEFING: GET GRANULAR

When preparing for a big event, whether it's a physically challenging task (say, a triathlon) or an emotional landmark (a wedding), it's important to visualize the experience with incredibly high attention to detail. Focusing only on the big things – such as the muscular or mental actions required to perform – might cause you to be thrown off-course by some of the smaller aspects of the challenge. As well as imagining the start line and finish of the race, the triathlete should also imagine seeing the crowds, smelling the sweat and experiencing the dressing room. The bride or groom should picture their breakfast and the car ride to church as much as they prepare for the exchange of vows.

A good example of this type of visualization would be the former Manchester United and England footballer Wayne Rooney. The night before a game, Rooney would speak to the kit man to learn the exact combination of kit colours the team were wearing the next day (sometimes the socks and shorts changed from one game to the next). With that intel, Rooney was able to visualize his ideal performance in sharp focus. I often did the same with my kit before missions, and I thought about how I was going to look as I swam through the water on a dive, or how my body would feel when attached to all sorts of equipment. It was as good as any training session.

It also helped to reconnect with my previous experience and past successes. Whenever I'm about to perform a tricky manoeuvre on *SAS: Who Dares Wins*, such as an insertion on to a fast-moving boat, I recall a time when I've done it for real: I remember how it feels to leave our own boat and scale a ladder on to the target vessel, all at speed. Recalling past successes was something our team leaders used to do before missions, too. Whenever a briefing session came to a close, it wasn't uncommon for someone to mention a similar operation that had ended well. Sometimes those recollections went all the way back to the Second World War, and they were designed to fill the lads with confidence.

The weird thing about visualization in my line of work was that it always had to be updated. Tactics changed. Kit changed. Technology changed. That meant I was always updating how I mentally rehearsed for jobs. In my first days of Royal Marines Basic Training, I remember being ordered to hold a weapon and crawl through the mud. I was told that whenever I needed to fire I would have to shout *BANG!* As I went to bed in the early days, this was the technique I relived in my head. Later, when we moved on to using blank ammo, my thinking changed, as it did once we moved on to live-round firing. Once I'd advanced to the elite level – running backwards, shooting shit in the pitch black, my head on a swivel – I upgraded my visualization yet again. With every switch, I altered the details in my preparation so everything would feel familiar. When it came to working with the new kit for real, I was more comfortable than I would have been had I gone in blindly.

→ THE LOOK FORWARD

Set yourself some time to visualize your mission and do it every day in granular detail. For example, if you're preparing for your driving test, see everything in advance, from the minute you arrive at the test centre. Drink the cheap coffee in the office, use the loo, say hello to your examiner. Walk through the car park to your vehicle, unlock the door, smell the air freshener, and hear the seatbelt zipping and clunking as you buckle up. From there, picture every manoeuvre running smoothly. Pro tip: throw a curveball into your thinking, like somebody crashing in front of you, but see yourself handling the incident efficiently. Don't dwell on it, though. Instead, live a successful test and move on.

CHAPTER 10
COMPETITION AS FUEL

As we rowed across the Atlantic in 2016, the work was a grind. The mission was for charity, so we had our motivation, but it was also an emotional headfuck that very nearly killed us. At times, our vessel, the *Elida*, tipped and yawed in the Atlantic swell like a piece of Lego in a bathtub. From inside the boat, I heard the water hammering against us as we pushed through a series of waves, some of which were around forty or fifty feet in height. I'd gawped up at them as our five-man crew worked through the day – tidal surges that reared up to the size of a building and collapsed with a furious crash. Having gone three weeks into an effort that would eventually last fifty days, all of us were sleep-deprived and knackered by the punishing rhythms of a work schedule that required us to row in shifts – two hours on, two hours off.

After one gruelling session on the oars it had been my time to rest, but as I stretched out in my bunk, the Atlantic's explosive power unsettled me. I was stuck in the dark, listening to the percussive, pounding water and imagining nature's fury outside.

Fucking hell, I thought. *This is not good.*

Fear was then replaced by regret. *What have we done?*

Sleeping proved almost impossible. And then I remembered: *Mate, you've chosen to be here.*

Like those moments of crisis I'd experienced in war, the fear and regret were fleeting. When my time to row eventually arrived, I switched on and got to work, powering through the water until I was exhausted. I'd then reset and go again – and again, and again. The other lads were feeling the same, so to take our minds off the stress of the deadly water around us, someone came up with the idea of a competition. We were a five-man team, with the boat set up to take two rowers at a time, but one of the lads brought a little rivalry to the event by achieving an impressive distance with a teammate and then challenging me and Aldo to beat it in the next shift.

'We're bigger than you,' he shouted. 'You're not going to be able to beat us on that!'

I knew all about the motivating factors associated with competition. In 1898, the US psychologist Norman Triplett published a study entitled *The Dynamogenic Factors in Pacemaking and Competition* in which he assessed children as they executed various tasks. His research showed that the kids performed faster when working near to another person than when operating solo. He also showed how a group of cyclists tended to move much faster than a solo rider and concluded the 'bodily presence of another contestant participating simultaneously in the race serves to liberate latent energy not ordinarily available'. In his research, Triplett acknowledged that shelter from the wind might have played a part in his results regarding a collective of cyclists, but he also suggested that encouragement and brain worry were other contributing factors.

Similarly, on the *Elida,* our teammate's challenge (within an already massive test) fired us up. For the next two hours, Aldo and myself goosed it, powering through the waves from 3 a.m. to sunrise while recording the longest distance during a shift. We had been so incentivized that nobody believed our results.

'There's no way you did that,' moaned one bloke.

'We fucking just did it! Look, there's the figures. You can't cheat the satnav, you bell-end!'

The challenge soon lost momentum, mainly because it was

limited in scope. There was only so long a test of distance could remain exciting within such a small group. However, as a lesson in the motivational power of competition, it proved eye-opening. By turning a rowing shift into a serious challenge, I'd felt compelled to push myself even harder. Had we persevered with it throughout the expedition, I reckon it might have been possible to shave another two days off our record-setting time.

TACTICAL BRIEFING: REWARD– COMPULSION LOOPS

A challenge of this kind is known as gamification, a term that describes an incentivized situation where the people involved are made to feel as if they're in a competitive event with rewards and prizes, rather than a god-awful, mind-numbing task, like rowing a boat across an ocean. Although it's a fairly modern term – thanks to its usage in a load of apps and gadgets, such as the Fitbit – gamification can really be traced back to groups like the Boy Scouts, who rewarded members with badges after they'd learned to master a certain skill (they still do). A modern equivalent would be the concept of 'streaks' on a website, in which a user is rewarded if they log in every day. Overall, gamification has been proven to promote positive behaviour, add interest or excitement to ordinarily boring events or activities, and present a route to success. That's because it taps into what's called a reward–compulsion loop, a feedback circuit known to release dopamine and encourage repeat performance.*

While the very undertaking of a mission is usually enough to keep a person inspired or motivated, there are times when fatigue,

* A quick note: these processes are fine if used sensibly. Just know that reward– compulsion loops have also been exploited by video game designers in order to motivate players. They're also indirectly attributed to some negative behaviours, such as gambling addiction.

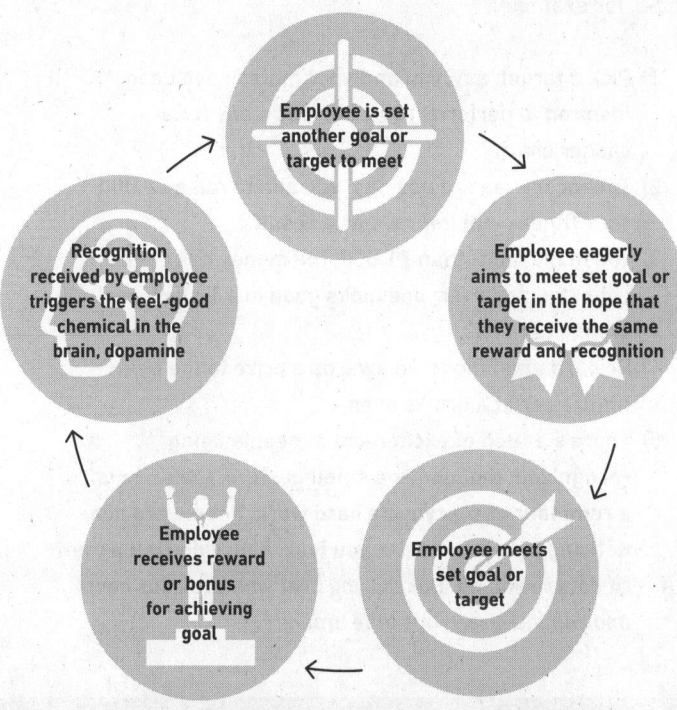

boredom or frustration can kick in, especially if the challenge is physically or mentally tough. It's in these situations that gamification can become particularly handy, as evidenced by our distance challenge on the Atlantic row. So, no matter the test, consider upping your productivity by modifying a reward–compulsion loop (such as the one above) and introducing gamification.

So, for example:

1) Pick a target: say, you and your mates have been inspired to perform 100 push-ups a day for a cancer charity.
2) The incentives are obvious: you aim to raise £1,000. Your fitness will improve as a result.
3) You make more than £1,500: the money has been collected and everyone looks good in a T-shirt. *Feels great, doesn't it?*
4) Reward time: the team awards a prize to the best fundraiser at a drinks event.
5) There's a rush of excitement at people being recognized: though it's a small gesture, the prize is a reminder of everyone's hard work. People are also noticing how much fitter you look. Fancy doing it again? Of course you do. *But can you beat your previous best and win the award this time around?*

⊕ THE LOOK FORWARD

Implement gamification to propel your mission, or add it to your day-to-day to encourage personal development. In a team event, reward individual success with awards, perks or prizes. If you're involved in a solo mission, celebrate an achievement (such as an improved personal best) with something that could be considered a treat.

CHAPTER 11
ARREST THE EGO

If you find yourself working with an egotist, it won't be a noticeable issue at first, for either the egotist or the people working around them. In many ways it's like having a tiny pebble stuck to the inside of your shoe: at first you'll barely notice it, but after a while the nagging sensation will grow into an annoyance. Finally, it will become so debilitating that simply putting one foot in front of the other feels almost impossible.

Don't believe me? Well, think of those three stages this way:

1) **An egotist has joined your team. Initially, their desire to be a driving force in the group feels exciting.**
2) **They start ignoring instructions. They shun advice. Resentment within the unit builds.**
3) **Unwilling to listen to orders (and believing they know best), the egotist behaves in a way that hinders the project. Arguments follow. The team ceases to function effectively.**

It's for this reason that I believe having a good sense of how the ego works is a vital resource. Over the years, I've come to recognize the ways in which an ego can put the individual – and, by extension, a mission – at risk of failure.

EGO IS AN AGENT OF CHAOS

Full disclosure: I have an ego, but, through military training, hard work and a series of humbling and educational failures, I'm currently able to keep a handle on it – most of the time. Quite recently, I was watching a war documentary that was being presented by a famous TV personality. The show was really good but the fact that the face of the show had zero military experience put me in a bad mood.

Why the fuck is he doing this?, I thought.

And then, *Why wasn't I asked to do it?*

That was my ego talking. I recognized the way in which it was driving my behaviour, and understanding that my moaning, ranting or sulking for days on end would lead to a bad outcome, I talked myself down.

'It doesn't need to be you on that show,' I said. 'You've got enough on your plate. And if you're really that bothered about missing out, how about you figure out some way of positioning yourself so you're in the frame next time?'

EGO IS A LEARNING KILLER

I see it all the time when filming *SAS: Who Dares Wins*. One of the recruits will screw up and the DS will point out what they're doing wrong, but rather than course-correcting, the recruit's ego will assure them that they know better than the DS. The recruit in question will then push ahead in a stubborn manner until they've either been yanked off the course or decided to withdraw voluntarily. They should be listening and learning, but instead their ego prevents them from doing so.

Whenever I've been involved in near-death scrapes in war, or even during some of my expeditions, I've always acknowledged my mistakes. I've assessed what's gone wrong and why. Then I've worked out how to avoid repeating the cock-up. That same process also takes place when things go well. Rather than backslapping my teammates, I say one simple thing to myself:

That worked out pretty good . . . But how can I make it work even better?

TACTICAL BRIEFING: MANAGING THE EGO

IF THE PROBLEM IS YOU

Maybe you've been told you have an ego problem. Or maybe you suspect that you do. Either way, the only way to solve the issue is to bring a little humility into your life. I suggest picking from one of the following ideas:

- Remember a time when you took a painful loss: I don't want you to dwell on the negative moments in your life for too long, but remembering a moment when you were brought down a notch or two – in work, business or life – will cool any delusions of grandeur. In a moment when you're tempted to act rashly, take a breath and recall this event.
- Volunteer: Donate your time to a valuable cause, because not only will it help you to feel gratitude for where you are in your life, it will distract you from the ego's biggest energy source: me, myself and I.
- Practice accountability: If you screw up, take an honest look at what happened. Then, accept ownership of the situation rather than looking to make excuses or blame others.

IF THE PROBLEM IS THEM

It might be that you're working with an alpha character or an egotistical personality and they're unwilling to listen to reason. If that's the case, I suggest the following:

- **Turn the egotist into an advantage.** You'll never win one over by asking them to consider what success might do for the mission as a whole. Instead, highlight what their performance will do for *them*. For example, you might be in a team bike race. Create a prize within your group that celebrates the fastest individual and watch the egotist give it everything.

- **Reframe your expectations.** If there's no way of bending the egotist to the mission's overall cause, it might help to shift your assumptions. A Billy Big-Bollocks won't accept responsibility (unless the outcome has been amazing), they won't show empathy, they won't behave with modesty and they definitely won't give themselves up for the greater good, so don't bother thinking they will.

- **Bin them.** An egotist can be a toxic presence. If you're in a position to give them the elbow, it might be a wise course of action.

→ THE LOOK FORWARD

Learn how to spot egotistical traits in yourself and others. Common signs include denial, a lack of empathy, holding grudges, a sense of entitlement, talking big without delivering, and a belief that the individual is better than everyone else. Unsure if you possess any of these traits? Send the list to your most trusted friends or colleagues and ask them to tick any that might be appropriate for you. Tell them they can reply anonymously if they want. (Be ready: this will encourage some brutal honesty.)

CHAPTER 12
REMEMBER THE PRIMARY MISSION

At this stage in the mission process, I'd like to throw in a very important reminder. *Remember the primary mission.* That's because, when conducting an operation or challenge of any kind, it can be very easy to lose sight of the overall objective. An illustration of this would be an individual hoping to shift a few stone through a combination of exercise and diet. What tends to happen is that they become so fixated on the smaller, 'mini missions' within their plan – gym class schedules, nutrition plans and sleeping routines – that they drift away from their priority: *the primary mission.* This is especially the case if they fail in some way, or an unexpected event slows their progress. It might be that they've missed a class, or fallen off the nutrition wagon for a day or two, but rather than seeing it as a small speed bump in an otherwise long journey, they regard the mistake as a detonation of the entire project. As a consequence they quit.

I've known not to treat the small hiccups as disasters because in the military all sorts of variables had the potential to throw a mission off-course. It might be that my unit had been tasked with picking up a person of interest, or raiding the compound of a known IED facilitator. Along the way, an operator could be killed in action, or seriously injured as they breached a door. It wasn't uncommon for a helicopter to break down, screwing up the team's original extraction method. But rather than becoming sidetracked, everyone in the British Armed Forces was trained to keep their focus on the primary mission, because not doing so usually led to failure.

Here's how it was done.

TACTICAL BRIEFING: FOCUS ON CLARITY

I've been in briefings for TV shows, media interviews and public appearances, and they don't hold a candle to the ones I witnessed during conflict. That's because in the military everything was so detailed. We were even presented with what were called 'warning orders' – a printed piece of paper that told us when and where the briefing was taking place, plus the people involved in the mission, the battle prep we needed to conduct in advance and a list of the kit and equipment required for the job. Finally, we were given a 'no-move before order', which meant that we weren't to go off site for any reason. (Not that we would.) Once the meeting had started, the preliminaries were addressed until we arrived at the core of the brief: the mission.

At this point, our *primary objective* would be stated. So, for example it might be that we had to smash up a heroin lab. This would be spelled out very clearly at the beginning, and it was regarded as the single most important part of the process because it gave us what we called our 'one up's intent' – or, in other words, what our bosses wanted us to achieve. 'It's *his* intent to smash up the heroin trade; it's *our* intent to smash up a heroin lab.' The primary objective was then stated again so it remained fixed in our minds, because what would follow was a lengthy description of the mission plan, and it was usually the most complicated part of the orders process.

I've learned from these briefings that if ever I have to come up with a mission statement of my own for a job or expedition, it has to be clearly defined and memorable. There's no point in me saying that I'm going to raise an unspecified amount of money for a charity in an unspecified amount of time. That won't focus me sufficiently; the primary mission can become lost in the vague logistics required to hit my goal. Instead, I'll get specific: 'I'm planning to raise £5,000 for charity in six weeks by racking up 1,000 miles on the bike, rower and treadmill.' That's usually enough to clarify the goal. Then I'll repeat the objective so it remains fixed.

A lot of individuals and industry leaders could learn from this process. I've presented talks on emotional resilience and structural organization to all sorts of businesses and I'm often amazed at just how overly complicated their mission statements are, and how their primary objectives can become lost over time. (It's not uncommon for a workforce to be entirely unknowing of their 'one-up's intent'.) The solution to this problem would be for these organizations to land upon a short and sweet primary objective that can be communicated throughout the company. That objective should then be repeated from time to time so that its importance isn't forgotten – because, as centuries of military procedure has shown, the clearer the mission brief, the greater its chances of success.

⊕ THE LOOK FORWARD

Throughout your mission, remind yourself of your primary objective. Make sure your intent is succinct and well defined. For instance:

- For two months I am drinking a maximum of five units of alcohol a week.
- I will conduct a personal finance audit on the 28th of every month.
- I am running three marathons in six months.

Make sure you repeat your intent over and over so that you don't become bogged down in the minutiae of the job in hand. If it helps, write the mission down on Post-it notes and stick them around your house, on your workstation and even put them in your kit bag.

CHAPTER 13
ANALYSE THE ENDING

Too often at the conclusion of a mission – as we blitz our way to the final minutes of a deadline, or towards the end of a 10K – we do so without absorbing the lessons that are being thrown at us. These moments can deliver the full gamut of emotions, from elation to pain, but if we don't stop to live them fully we won't a) reap the full benefit of the situation we've survived or b) fully understand the message those emotions and experiences are trying to convey to us. The trick is to sprint the final yards with our heads up, eyes open.

I know I've been guilty of rushing through the end of missions in the past. When I kayaked down the Yukon in 2019, the last few days were a headfuck. Our time was tight – we had a flight to catch, and the financial costs of missing it were huge; I also had a work project to think about on the other side of the trip, and at times I was unable to fully immerse myself in the fact that I was living in nature and surrounded by some awe-inspiring scenery. With hindsight, I should have acknowledged the precariousness of the situation and then made the best of what it had to offer.

That was an anomaly for me. When it comes to concluding a mission, I've long known that absorbing the horrendous moments can carry a lot of value. I've been on expeditions where the process of simply keeping my head above water has felt like a struggle. It was the same on some of my military operations: there were jobs that went wrong, where mistakes were made and life became incredibly hectic in an instant. But rather than shutting out the discomfort, I tried to take mental notes of the hurt because it sometimes delivered valuable intelligence on my working practices later down the line.

I've recently made it a habit to carve out some time at the end of a mission to soak up the moment. A recent shoot for *SAS: Who Dares Wins* took place in Vietnam and as the work drew to a close, I made a concerted effort to carve out some alone-time; every now and then, during a break in filming, I walked away to take in the jungle scenery. It helped me to appreciate what was going on in the project. I analysed the relationships I'd built within the team and my performance. I even gained a greater appreciation of what I needed in life to be happy.

Even if I lost everything, it wouldn't be that bad, I thought. *I came from nothing, so if I have to go back to nothing, I'll be alright . . .*

None of that would have happened if I'd been racing towards the end, my head down, living in the future.

TACTICAL BRIEFING: EMOTIONS ARE COMBAT INDICATORS

Emotions are what get most people into trouble. They lead us into making bad decisions in all manner of situations, whether phys-ically, romantically, financially, legally, creatively . . . The list goes on and on. But emotions aren't in place to cause trouble; they're supposed to act as a guide. Sadly for a lot of people, simply under-standing how we're feeling, and why, is a massive conundrum. As a result we misinterpret what we're experiencing and react in the wrong way.

In my opinion emotions are combat indicators, a signal that some dynamic situation – positive or negative – is approaching. The trick is to accurately interpret what those emotions are telling us and then respond accordingly.

Some feelings are easy to unpack:

- I'm angry because some bell-end has cut me up on the road.
- I'm on a downer because I'm not over my ex.
- I'm excited because I've landed a new job.

Others are much trickier to untangle, and the most complicated of these is anxiety. This is a feeling that can sit in the guts for days, gnawing at a person's subconscious without fully revealing the root cause. Example: you're about to embark on a physical challenge abroad, but you've picked up a worrying injury. Rather than acknowledging the lack of fitness, your anxious mind is finding other things to stress about, such as the finances of the trip, a logistical issue or some personality clash among the people you're travelling with. But after a while, and a little digging, the truth eventually emerges: you're anxious because you're not fit and admitting the truth might kibosh the trip.

In uncomfortable situations where your emotions aren't clearly defined, it's best to first accept that you're feeling anxious and then trust that the root cause will surface with time. Then drill into the situation with a few questions:

1) **'What am I feeling?'**
   Stress.
2) **'Why am I feeling that way?'**
   I feel overworked. Someone has pointed out my latest project is behind schedule and it's bothering me.
3) **'Where is that feeling coming from?'**
   I'm not as experienced in my position as I would like to be and those comments have pricked at my insecurities.

It's in these psychological explorations that we can a) learn about the true cause of our feelings and b) find a way of negating them. From there we can truly appreciate the results of our latest mission.

⊕ THE LOOK FORWARD

To get into the habit of making the most of a concluding mission, make a note of your emotions at the beginning (or end) of every day. At times the process will feel hectic; on other occasions it will seem pointless, especially if you're feeling great at the time. But by committing yourself to this exercise, self-assessing your psychological state in times of stress will become almost second nature. When those stressful moments arrive at the conclusion to a mission, you'll know exactly how to interpret your emotions. From there you can self-improve, using any knowledge you might have gained.

PART TWO:
RECOVERY

INTRODUCTION

At the conclusion of every mission, or challenging life event, it's important we take some time to recover. It might be that your life had briefly turned into a proper shitshow – you've got divorced, fallen seriously ill or lost your job. Maybe the opposite has happened and you've reached a massive milestone in life – you've graduated from uni, got married or had a baby. Either way, your head's probably in a bit of a spin with emotion. Sadness. Pride. Excitement. Grief. Worry. Guilt. Happiness. Anger . . . *All of it.* Your body might feel knackered, too; tactically you might be all over the shop. The challenge now is to adjust quickly because life is like an enemy force in a dynamic conflict – it won't sit back for a breather just because you're tired. Instead, it's more likely to smack you in the mouth with a succession of hits: new deadlines, physical challenges, bills, train journeys, work issues, disputes, family commitments and all. If you don't make a decent recovery from your latest test, there's every chance something might trip you up.

In the military elite I was always encouraged to manage my recovery periods effectively so I could return to the thick of it feeling 100 per cent. This was done through a variety of processes. Firstly, a brief holiday was encouraged – that's if I felt like it, though I rarely did and I usually stayed at home and went on the beers with mates. A couple of weeks later, I was expected back at base, where I worked on a series of training exercises so my skill sets could be brought up to date. I was also rolled into any UK-based operations that might have been going on at the time. During this period I made sure to keep myself physically sharp in the gym because I always wanted my performance levels to be at their maximum, ready for when I was sent back into the fight.

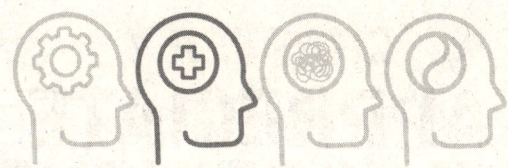

The one area I overlooked during these recovery periods was my mind – the most important resource we have. I witnessed some horrific things in war. On a nightly basis I was exposed to the type of stress levels that might emotionally crush an untrained individual, but because I'd been prepared for it, I was able to come through most of those experiences unscathed – most, but not all, and I rarely acknowledged any low-level trauma I was feeling. The long-term impact was like death by a thousand cuts and when I eventually realized I was in emotional pain, I had no idea why it was happening – even though it should have been obvious – or what I needed to do about it. A near-fatal breakdown followed by a successful period of therapy has since opened up an armoury of tools that I can now use to ensure I recover properly from any mission, or dramatic life experience, whether that's a highly risky expedition to the scenic arse-end of nowhere or some time spent healing from a broken leg.

A lot of people struggle to recover fully from their most recent challenges. Not decompressing efficiently, or failing to restore their energy levels in a productive manner, leaves them vulnerable to future stresses and potential failure. At the very least, they'll feel shittier for much longer. Decompression is a discipline, and if applied properly, the following physical, mental and technical weapons will ensure the user returns to their optimum self much more adeptly. And there's a good chance they'll feel even stronger than before.

Who ever thought that resting could be so productive?

CHAPTER 1
APPRECIATE THE EXPERIENCE

In the hours and days that follow an impactful life event it's vital we appreciate the experience for what it was. Maybe we've failed in some way, in which case it's a benefit to sit with any negative emotions so that they can be used to fire us up for the next challenge. Following moments of success, it's a long-term help to relive any positive feelings because they can be weaponized for when life gets noisy again. These days, my aim at the end of every job is to buzz off the highs and ride the lows while they're fresh so they can be turned into a resource. After all, what's the point in doing a mission in the first place if you're not going to grow from it?

This should be a habitual process for us all, no matter the project. For example, if we've failed an exam, we should take a moment to feel the disappointment. If we've just won a sporting competition, we should celebrate the success and appreciate the efforts involved. During the more hectic stages of my military life I didn't run through this process and in the end it screwed me up. After returning home from tours, I found it particularly hard to process what had happened to me because the memories weren't as vivid. Later, once I'd fallen apart, that meant I couldn't work out exactly why.

That all changed following a period of therapy, and these days I'll sit with my experiences after a mission because there's often so much chaos to take in. For example, while kayaking down the Yukon, we were chased by a grizzly bear on a riverbank and had to sit in our kayaks until it had buggered off. Shortly afterwards we were almost wiped out by a series of churning rapids that came out of nowhere. We turned our kayaks broadside, hoping the whitecaps wouldn't upend us. Then we entered into the churn, somehow making it through to the other side without capsizing or losing any supplies.

Once I'd eventually boarded the plane home (following the mission's hectic conclusion), I flicked through the photos on my phone and watched the hours of video I'd recorded. There was a sense of pride: I'd overcome some of the most difficult circumstances Mother Nature could throw at a person. The cold, the wet, the rapids . . . *Even a bloody bear*. My resilience had been tested to the limits in an uncompromising challenge and I'd emerged unscathed. I had every right to feel good about myself. By the expedition's end I'd also realized that my experience had been unique to me. Nobody else had gone through the exact same journey, in much the same way that your missions – and the emotions they'll throw up – will be uniquely yours.

My flight home took me from Anchorage to Seattle and I was able to see the Yukon from my window seat. As I looked down at the vast meandering turns that stretched into the distance, and where the river broke off in different directions, I made sure to tap into my overwhelming feelings. I experienced a powerful sense of awe.

Fuck, that was incredible, I thought.

Then I felt a pang of FOMO. *We hadn't seen half of it*. My emotional position told me what I had to do to overcome that feeling.

Try something else. Just more epic.

TACTICAL BRIEFING: MANAGE THE COMEDOWN

Taking some time to appreciate your most recent challenge is a pretty good pathfinder for your next steps. I'm not saying that you should immediately drill down into what went wrong and what went right; where you screwed up and where you overachieved. That takes place closely after. What I am saying is that you should feel what has taken place, because too often we push on to the next challenge or the next deadline without really absorbing what we've been through, not to mention the impact our mission might have had on us and on the people we're close to.

From my experience, finishing an expedition and re-entering a period of normality can sometimes feel like a comedown. For example, when I've completed filming with the lads on *SAS: Who Dares Wins* there's always a high – the adrenaline peaks; I feel euphoric and excited – and having it suddenly stripped away is probably what a junkie experiences when they go cold turkey. I feel a void; there's a dramatic shift in the pace of life – but the only way to overcome that sensation is to reflect once a mission is completed. This allows me to manage the comedown and make sense of it, rather than making a crash landing.

The alternative is to rush back into normal life full speed, and the consequences can be turbulent. For example, say your mission has been life-changing in some way: you might feel anger that no one is truly appreciating your experience or achievements, and there might be some frustration at the slower pace of your new normal. Then there are the personalities around you. People are peculiar – they can become resentful when somebody succeeds and a toxic personality might attempt to diminish your results with a series of shitty comments or a few jokes. (My suggestion would be to cut a person like that out of your life.) Full disclosure: I know that I can get a bit moody if my partner has been away on an exciting work trip. I feel a little jealous at not having a fulfilling experience of my own, and likewise she can be the same with me. It's something we're working on.

All of this can be negotiated if we take some time to appreciate the confusing feelings that sometimes land after a mission. You'll find value in them. At the very least, you'll discover what you like and don't like. It won't give you all the answers and there might be some serious stuff to work through, but appreciating everything you've experienced, while being honest about the emotional fall-out, should ensure you won't come down with a bump.

⊖ THE LOOK FORWARD

Following your next mission – big or small – really enjoy your achievements, or lick your wounds if things haven't gone so well. This can be a team effort, too. If you have a significant other, or a person you live or work with, process the experience with them.

EXAMPLE

It might be that you and your partner have just moved house. As the dust settles on the upheaval, appreciate that you've both gone through a challenging life event and dig into how you both feel about it. Acknowledgement will help you to find a new normal more quickly than if you carry on as if nothing has happened.

CHAPTER 2
TAKE A LONG, HARD LOOK

The world of the military operator isn't an egotistical environment, despite the fact it's often dominated by alpha-male types. For the most part, a sense of humility is found within most elite units, which is important because it enables some unflinching self-analysis when things have gone wrong. In the aftermath of negative and positive actions, we always asked painful questions of one another; the fuck-ups were pointed out and any individuals who might have slipped up in some way were criticized, even after a successful conclusion. No stone was left unturned, hurt feelings counted for shit, and everyone involved would have a say. There was generally a level of calm during these situations because a Tier One individual knew not to rant and rave at anyone who might have screwed up. Instead it was our job to acknowledge any errors and improve. Having a frank and open appraisal was the only way to learn and grow.

The perfect time to conduct these meetings was during a period of recovery, in the minutes immediately after an operation or training exercise had concluded. (Your circumstances might not allow such a timeframe, but I do recommend conducting a post-operational debrief ASAP.) The reasons for working this way were clear:

- Only by appreciating a mission for what it was, in the

immediate aftermath, could we get a handle on the tiny details that might later fade from the memory. Our appraisals were immediate and dynamic; there was no point in us discussing our activities over a brew and Post-it notes a week down the line.

- Analysis of both the group and the individual was required because we all understood that the only way to stay ahead of our enemy was to learn and improve, using what we knew about them and about ourselves.

Once brought together, the group pooled all the resources available, including human intelligence (HUMINT), which included eye-witness reports, air and ground surveillance, and technology such as headcam footage and intercepted communications. All of this was then assessed in order to develop a clear picture of exactly what had taken place.

I can count on a single finger the times my team *didn't* assess our missions, and this process isn't confined to the military world – it takes place in the top tiers of business, finance, sport, entertainment and public services, such as the fire brigade or police. In all industries, the best of the best have long understood that to stay ahead of the competition it's important to learn from any mistakes and build upon the successes, while adapting to any changes or new challenges in the field. The only way to do that is to self-analyse, over and over, and then act on the lessons learned.

The most important component in this process is honesty. There's no point covering up any blunders you might have made. Likewise, you shouldn't let a colleague off the hook if they're usually a solid character, because a) it won't help the group in the long run, and b) there's a good chance another operator will call you out on your bullshit attitude. One person who's particularly good at this is my *SAS: Who Dares Wins* mate Mark 'Billy' Billingham. Billy is under no illusion that he's fallible; he knows he can make errors, but that he'll learn from them – his motto is 'Always a little further' for a reason. If Billy does fail while filming, for whatever reason, he will raise his hands during our regular debriefs. Though we're mates, he'll also have a pop at me if I've ballsed up, but that's because it's the only way for us to improve.

TACTICAL BRIEFING: HOW TO CONDUCT AN EXTREME SELF-ANALYSIS

It's time to buckle up, because you're about to give yourself a roasting.

At the end of every mission, as we recover and regroup, it's important to debrief as soon as possible, no matter how painful or pointless the process might feel. By allowing time to pass, you'll only forget the details, so the sooner you get your thoughts down the better (and those of your team, if the mission was a shared activity). I always start the process by asking myself a series of questions:

1) 'Overall, am I pleased with my performance?'
2) 'What went wrong and why?'
3) 'What lessons can I draw from that experience? *How can I improve?*'
4) 'What am I pleased with?'
5) 'Why did I succeed in that area? Again: *How can I improve?*'
6) 'Emotionally, how am I?'
7) 'Are those emotions something I need to take care of? If so, how? Finally: *How can I improve?*'

There's really no point my living in self-denial or answering the questions dishonestly, because it's only going to bite me on the arse at some point. In my previous job, that attitude might have cost a life – either a teammate's or my own – whereas in my current profession, a slack attitude to self-analysis could cause me to get injured or I might be viewed as a liability by my clients. So, I won't go gently. Even during my early days of serving at the sharp end of war, I was overly critical of my performances, which was a factor that allowed me to stay out of too much trouble. I can vividly recall one training session where I struggled to scale a caving ladder. As I flapped about on the rungs, some of the other lads took a pop at me, which really pissed me off. When I got back to base that day, I took a long, hard look at myself.

'Overall, am I pleased with my performance?'

No. I was shit today. I couldn't seem to get my technique right and physically I was blowing.

'What went wrong and why?'

I felt out of my depth on the ladder. Maybe I hadn't prepared properly: I've only just started this type of training, so the technique will come eventually, but I've got to square it away soon because the other lads have eyes on me now. They'll be watching to see how I react.

'What lessons can I draw from that experience?'

I need to work on my ladder-climbing! I also understand that failure, even in the new operators, won't be tolerated here. I have to be on the ball in everything I do.

'How can I improve?'

I can climb more ladders. Working on my upper-body strength will also help with the physical aspects of the task. Mentally I need to understand that criticism and the constant pursuit of excellence is part of the job.

'Emotionally, how am I?'

Pissed off at taking a bit of stick. Annoyed that I couldn't get it right. A little anxious that I might struggle to course-correct.

'Are those emotions something I need to take care of? If so, how?'

Not at the moment. Rather than catastrophizing, I can turn the negatives into positives by using anger, annoyance and anxiety as motivators when I next train.

I self-analysed and drilled down into what I was getting wrong and why. The process didn't take long – maybe five to ten minutes. Then I worked on turning the situation around. I went to the gym; I practised the various climbing techniques, again and again, and my performances noticeably improved. In the end, the incident proved to be both a major kick up the arse and a valuable lesson. When it comes to self-improvement, the only way an individual will ever get to fully understand their strengths and weaknesses is by running through a regular period of self-analysis during their recovery periods. If done fully and honestly, an uptick in performance will surely follow.

⊙ THE LOOK FORWARD

Conduct a self-analysis of your latest project. Answer the questions honestly and don't hold back. As with some other tasks in this book, if you want an unflinching appraisal of your efforts, hand these questions to a colleague or friend to answer for you. Remember not to take it personally when you hear things you don't like, which you inevitably will. Instead, try your best to reframe any criticism as an opportunity to improve.

CHAPTER 3
ESTABLISH YOUR OFF-CYCLE

During periods of recovery it can be tempting to drift, take the foot off the gas entirely and overly bask in the afterglow of success – or wallow in the pain of self-pity. In reality, while rest and recuperation are major priorities when decompressing, this doesn't mean an individual should abandon all responsibility or lose sight of the things that made them successful in the first place. Instead, it's important to create a semblance of regularity so that life doesn't go haywire.

Mistakes were made following the first season of *SAS: Who Dares Wins*. I was a bit of a twat to be around after the first few shows had gone out. I'd opened myself up publicly on some of the emotional struggles I'd endured in life and I felt exposed. The other problem was that I'd had a taste of something good. I was on TV, I had money in the bank and I was going out a lot, usually until silly o'clock, and then not waking up until midday. As a consequence, I wasn't training right, eating right or sleeping right, which only worsened my state of mind. At a point in my life when I should have been feeling great and smashing my targets, I actually felt pretty lousy.

This was totally different from my periods of downtime in the military because, really, there were very few moments then when there *wasn't* anything to do. Yes, we were encouraged to recharge whenever we came off a tour abroad, but after a week or two of holiday, there were always plenty of tasks to perform. Usually these were training- or surveillance-related, and the onus was always on us to stay physically and mentally sharp. With hindsight, these schedules were in place to maximize our talents and up-grade our skill sets while we were away from the actual business of fighting. But they also prevented us from drifting, losing focus and going off the boil.

These days, I have a whole new attitude to the business of re-covery or 'off-cycling'. In fact, I tend to structure my life so rigidly during these periods that it's almost like I haven't got an off-cycle at all. I train every day if I can. I work. I make sure to eat right and recover right. All of these things tend to place me in the right frame of mind for when the chaos inevitably hits again – either through work or some other issue. Of course, those hectic moments are no way near as stressful as my time in war, but it's all relevant, isn't it? Feeling the fear as I abseil down the face of a dam is no different from the fear I experienced whenever an IED went off: I was scared of dying. With a maximized off-cycle in place, I've since been able to remain resolute and get the job done in my new career, too.

TACTICAL BRIEFING: SETTING MILESTONES

It's only natural that building a productive off-cycle should feel like an overwhelming task. During recovery, moving into a phase of productivity can seem like a ball-ache. However, I've found that one way of kick-starting the process is to set up a series of reachable milestones throughout the day. The primary purpose of this is to stay productive until the time arrives for you to revert to your on-cycle, or normal routine. But it can also deliver a sense of achievement as you do so. Ticking jobs off a list gives us a shot of dopamine and improves our well-being. Why else do you think business leaders encourage us to deal with emails and manage-able admin first thing in the morning?

Experience has also taught me that a person can be locked into an ever-decreasing circle of unproductive behaviour when a day passes them by. That's why I like to hit a timetable of milestones once I've entered into my off-cycle, some of which are easy to achieve – like eating breakfast and hydrating properly – while others require a lot more effort, such as training for or researching my next project. Once I've nailed one, I'll cross it off a list, making sure to celebrate each achievement as I go along. I've found that running through this process creates a headspace in which I feel productive and mentally engaged with what's going on around me. The alternative is to slump on the sofa and gawp at Instagram for hours.

One trick I've learned during this off-cycle stage is that it's important not to set too many rigid deadlines. Yes, you want to get shit done during the day, but you shouldn't beat yourself up if a legitimate distraction presents itself or your plans go awry for whatever reason. Rather than writing up a timetable of non-negotiable targets and times, I'll work to a flexible schedule knowing that if things go askew, I can still achieve all my aims. For example, rather than stating that I'm going to train by 10 a.m., I'll simply keep in mind that I'm going to work out some time in the morning. That way, if I do get ahead of myself, I can feel like I'm on top of my game again; if I don't, I won't become disheartened or feel like I'm going off-track.

Remember, during phases of recovery it's vital that we ease back to 100 per cent with patience and self-care. Giving yourself an emotional beasting because you didn't land all your goals during a set period won't get you to where you want to be. By approaching the process carefully there should be enough structure in your off-cycle to both heal and return to full strength so you can deal with the onslaught when it inevitably arrives again.

⊕ THE LOOK FORWARD

Plan a daily and weekly schedule of tasks that will a) help return you to your optimum fitness levels, and b) keep your head in the game by maintaining some level of productivity.

EXAMPLE

You've returned to a normal work schedule following a vital project, where late nights and stressed weekends have become the unhealthy norm. During the off-cycle, recover fully with a period of recuperation, which could include a productive and relaxing wind-down schedule (favourite TV shows, reading, cooking new meals), an inspiring activity (golf, strength training, something creative), or a relaxing weekend with friends and family. At the same time, conduct a brief catch-up period at work so you can check in with any commitments that might have been temporarily put to one side during your hectic phase and assess the performance levels of your teammates.

CHAPTER 4
OWN YOUR SCREW-UPS

There's a saying in the tech industry that start-up businesses should 'fail fast and fail forward'. By that, it's meant that a) a new company needs to get its mistakes out of the way early, and b) it has to learn from those mistakes by extracting as much intelligence from them as possible. The British military thinks in pretty much the same way. It's probably for this reason that it's long been regarded as one of the best fighting forces in the world when it comes to operational flexibility, and from my experience that's because:

- For hundreds of years, it has asked the question:
  'How can we do better?'
- When tactical screw-ups are made, it owns them immediately and course-corrects.
- It rarely assumes to know everything, because that would only lead to disaster.

Let me illustrate the power of these combined approaches by taking an example from recent global events and showing you how *not* to fail. For this little exercise we're going to look at Russia, a force that was once feared around the world due to its military might, but was recently given a bloody nose by Ukraine following Vladimir Putin's 2022 invasion of their territory. After the shock and awe of Russia's early incursions, their military advances were repelled and Ukraine kicked back hard. Putin's invasion became bogged down. At points, Ukrainian forces were executing raids on Russian territory and seriously impacting their infrastructure. The weird thing is, almost from the beginning of the conflict most of the flaws in Russia's offensive were obvious for everyone to see. And yet they seemed unwilling, or unable, to do something about them. If anything, they were failing backwards, and failing slowly.

The reasons for this were clear. Over the last century, Russia had constructed a rigid and archaic military doctrine for itself without moving with the times. As a result, its systems had become outdated, and any mistakes it may have made – a series of lessons it could have learned from – were overlooked. Rather than acknowledging that their initial battle plan hadn't worked, Russia's military leaders held fast – and suffered. Their forces sustained heavy losses. Worse, there was very little transparency about what was taking place, which only confused matters for those involved. It soon became clear that the soldiers scrapping on the ground were without communications and their logistical supply chains had taken a kicking. Suddenly, Russia's forward-projected troops were without food, water and fuel. Cold, tired and vulnerable, their morale quickly fell apart and the military campaign slowed considerably. But had they admitted to their errors in the early stages of the war, it might have been a whole other story.

Handily, we can all learn from their screw-up.

TACTICAL BRIEFING: WRITE YOUR OWN STANDARD OPERATING PROCEDURE

In the British Armed Forces, a Standard Operating Procedure, or SOP, is a set of guidelines that accompanies just about every routine process that an individual or team will complete on the ground – either in combat or peacetime. Drawn up as instructions to be followed step by step, the SOP's aim is to simplify important tasks that might otherwise feel overwhelming as a whole. They're also flexible. The minute one of them becomes outdated, or inefficient, its flaws are acknowledged and the SOP is immediately rewritten.

However, a document of this kind isn't effective only in war. It's an asset for just about anyone engaged in an activity that requires excellence and consistency. For example, imagine a company boss looking to hire a new member of staff. An SOP for this process could run as follows:

- **Step One:** Imagine the perfect hire. Detail their key attributes.
- **Step Two:** With those attributes in mind, draw up a longlist of the ten best candidates for interview.
- **Step Three:** Conduct reconnaissance by digging into each candidate's CV, references and social media profile (don't get too creepy here).
- **Step Four:** Have a series of set questions for each candidate.
- **Step Five:** After the first round of interviews, draw up a shortlist of the three best candidates.
- **Step Six:** Conduct a second interview for the three best candidates and hire the top choice.

For the most part, a system of this kind will run smoothly, though should things go haywire or become out of date, the SOP can be rewritten. (Often this is done in the aftermath, when things have calmed down.) In the example outlined here, it might be that trawling through a candidate's entire social media profile creates too many confusing and/or biased sets of data. Instead, the interviewer should admit their mistake, rewrite the SOP and adapt the next search to work-related resources only, such as LinkedIn.

You should take the same approach in your life. During the

Recovery phase, acknowledge any mission-related blunders you may have made and course-correct. It's the only way to stay on track when committing to the continual pursuit of excellence.

⊕ THE LOOK FORWARD

For fun, write a couple of Standard Operating Procedures for some of the regular activities in your life. Potential targets could include:

- Your gym routine, complete with warm-up drills and exercises, plus reps, sets, weights, distances, etc.
- A regular work activity, such as the conducting of staff appraisals or the writing of annual reports.
- Your weekly food shop. Make sure to include a list of regular items, the ideal time for shopping and the average bill. Also run an inventory on which food items incur the most wastage, so you can reduce them in the next shop. And the items that run out too quickly, so you can increase them.

By building a step-by-step instructional guide on your regular activities, it's possible to ensure consistently positive results. And remember: if things go wrong at any point, fail fast and fail forward by rewriting the SOP.

CHAPTER 5
RESET YOUR FOUNDATIONS

There's no point expecting your world to return to normal immediately during a period of recovery, especially not after a gruelling mission of some kind. No one wanders through the Amazon jungle and returns to a city life as if nothing much has happened. There will be fatigue, a changed sense of perspective, and maybe a renewed enthusiasm for some cause (an ecological charity) or activity (exploration). The same applies if you've just had a kid, started a new business or lost a loved one: there are likely to be huge shifts – some of them mental, some physical – and, if left unmanaged, any temporary negative symptoms might turn chronic.

In these moments it's important we connect to the foundations in our lives, so we can decompress and reset fully while going about our normal day-to-day. While the completion of some life-altering adventure should always be celebrated, it's unlikely the boss is going to be happy if we've decided to kick back in the office in order to recover. The same can be said of grief. This can be a crippling, unseen pain, but there comes a point where we all have to slip back into normality in order to move forward. In both situations, finding a solid footing on which to recover is a priority if we're not to experience any long-term damage.

To succeed it's important we solidify our emotional and physical well-being. The US psychologist and author Phil Stutz best explained this process during his Netflix documentary *Stutz* – a film based around his sessions with the actor Jonah Hill. In it, Stutz discusses the concept of 'life force', a pyramid comprising three building blocks that he uses to create personal stability during a time of crisis: 'The only way to find out what you should be doing, like who you are, is to activate your life force, because your life force is the only part of you that actually is capable of guiding you when you're lost. If you think of it as a pyramid, there are three levels of the life force. The bottom level is your relationship with your physical body. The second layer is your relationship with other people. And the highest level is your relationship with yourself.'

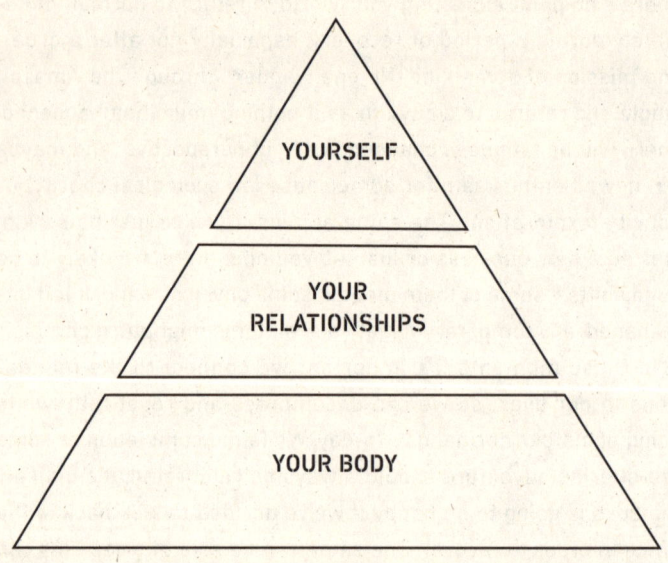

In the pyramid, the bottom block is the widest: Stutz reckons that a person's life force can improve by 85 per cent simply by looking after the physical state with exercise, nutrition and the right levels of sleep. The next layer involves connecting with others and contributes 10 per cent of life force. The top level, which requires a person to check in on the self, delivers the final 5 per cent.

Coincidentally I've unconsciously applied this same idea during my periods of recovery, in the following ways:

- **Physical:** Following a trip away, I ease into my new routine by returning to a healthy pattern of sleep, winding down and waking up in the right way. I'll return to the gym as soon as I'm ready, though I always listen to my body in order not to overdo it or injure myself. I also supplement my physical work with a solid nutrition plan.
- **People:** I'll make sure to spend time with friends and family during this period. I'll share my experiences with the people I care about, talk through any issues I might have noticed and reconnect with my brotherhood (a term I've often used to describe my friendship group).
- **Self:** Every day I check in with how I'm feeling – good, bad, ugly. I'll also do things that make me feel grounded and happy. I'll hang out with my partner, watch sport on the telly and spend a healthy amount of time outdoors.

Depending on the length and personal impact of the mission, this process can take anywhere from a day or two to a couple of weeks to complete. Once it's finished and my foundations have been reset, the world around me tends to feel a whole lot steadier. Then I plan and go again.

TACTICAL BRIEFING: BUILD YOUR PYRAMID

The idea of resetting our foundations is something we should all subscribe to. In fact, I'd go as far as to say it should be a habitual process. Too often we thrash our bodies and minds without giving any thought as to what might happen afterwards, other than the rewards it might bring. I don't care what you're doing. It might be a stressful work project, a weight-loss programme or a family issue that needs resolving: your life will likely feel very different in the aftermath and the quickest way to locate a new normal is to find stability. Here's how you're going to do it:

REBUILD: EXERCISE. EVERY DAY.

I'm not ordering you to smash out 100 push-ups before breakfast, deadlift a personal best or run a marathon. Instead, try to fall back into a familiar programme that's suitable and rewarding for you. (This is not the time to take up a martial art or an extreme sport.) Walk. Swim. Stretch. Hit the gym, play football or go rock climbing. Whatever floats your boat, *do it*; just get the body moving every twenty-four hours. When it comes to nutrition, eat clean, cut out the alcohol and maybe try intermittent fasting. Then get the recommended eight hours of sleep a night. This can be achieved by doing the following:

- Live by the '3–2–1' sleep rule: stop eating three hours before bed; stop drinking two hours before bed; turn off the phone one hour before bed.
- No caffeine after lunch.
- Go to bed and wake up at regular times.
- Before sleeping, meditate, plan the following day or read.

BROTHERHOOD/SISTERHOOD: WHO'S YOUR TRIBE?

At the end of a mission, meet with friends and family as soon as you can. Celebrate; commiserate. There's every chance you'll have some stories to share, so express them. The people you love are a great resource when it comes to processing your experience – at the very least, you'll get to see it from a different perspective. At the same time, your brother- or sisterhood will serve as a distraction from whatever it is you've been through, while helping you to reconnect with normality. Just ensure these connections align with your rebuild. Going out and smashing ten pints every night won't help you to reset. In fact, it will set you back.

SELF-CARE: TAKE A PERSONAL MOT.

This works in two ways. The first is to check in with your headspace every day. You can do this by writing down your thoughts for a few minutes in the morning, or saying them out loud when you're alone. This can help you to find some clarity on your emotional state. The second method is to psychologically recover by rewarding yourself after all that bloody hard work. Take a few days off. Eat your favourite meal. Go to the football. Whatever's going to make you feel happy, *do it*.

⊕ THE LOOK FORWARD

Draw your pyramid. Fill it with the things you know will help you to find stable ground in the days and weeks after your mission has concluded. Don't worry about my choices when it comes to doing this task – *your pyramid is 100 per cent personal*. So if you want to cycle through the woods, chat to your next-door neighbour over the fence or smash out a sunrise workout every morning, *go for it*. The important thing is that you look after yourself and find stability. From there you can make a steady next step.

CHAPTER 6
LIVE A PARALLEL LIFE

Imagine if you could live your life twice: at the exact same time, but in two very different ways. In Life A, you've become a bag of shit, having neglected your well-being and fitness, not to mention your family and work commitments, and your social circle. On the other hand, in Life B, you've trained to stay healthy, both physically and mentally, and as a result you have a solid connection with work, money and everyone around you. During both journeys the big things happen in exactly the same way – there are births and deaths, marriages and divorces, and career successes and disasters – but that's where the similarities end: experience has taught me that the individuals working through Life B rather than Life A will recover more quickly and more effectively from a seismic event because they've been prepared for it.

In times of recovery, if ever I find myself unable to get back into a decent routine, I imagine these two parallel lives at work. I see the one in which I'm on top form, fit and sparking; and the other, where I'm not. I visualize one of those big life events happening, like a job offer or a family tragedy, and then I see myself functioning in both. In Life A, I'm not up to speed because I haven't been taking care of my body or my head. In Life B, I feel strong and sharp, and I'm able to effectively maximize opportunity or handle adversity. This exercise is usually a good motivator when I'm working my way back to full strength, because the difference in perceived outcomes is so stark. By briefly picturing the negative results of a less disciplined lifestyle, I'll find the impetus to work even harder.

You don't have to use this technique in such a dramatic way (though I'd definitely recommend it). Seeing a parallel life can be just as effective when assessing the smaller events in our daily routines. For example, consider how both lives A and B might work when the alarm clock goes off in the morning:

- **Life A: Wakey-wakey!** You check the phone for texts and social media, and make coffee before doom-scrolling and looking at Instagram for another thirty minutes. Finally you make breakfast, get ready and go to work.
- **Life B: Wakey-wakey!** You check in with your feelings, run through a quick gratitude meditation, stretch and smash out fifty push-ups. Finally, you eat breakfast (which has been prepped the night before), get ready and go to work.

Life A or Life B: which do you think is more likely to see you fired up for the challenges ahead?

Now seize the day.

TACTICAL BRIEFING: DON'T BEAT YOURSELF UP FOR PAST MISTAKES

When imagining these parallel lives, it's easy to get into a bit of a state about what you could or should have done in the past, especially when it comes to the issues of money, health, relationships or lifestyle:

- What if I hadn't bought a coffee on the way to work every day for the last five years? I'd have saved thousands!

- What if I'd done intermittent fasting/gone to a therapist/joined a running club sooner? I'd be so much better off.
- What if I hadn't wasted my time with this toxic person or that miserable job? I'd be a lot happier today.

Considering life in this way is a waste of time, because there's no tactical advantage to it. Sure, appreciate the sting of disappointment, but given that there's no way of turning back the clock, my advice is to use any negative experiences as fuel. It's not easy, but I've learned that if I start viewing my past mistakes in this way, it helps if I then reframe my mood in the following three stages:

1) **Acknowledge:** I tell myself I've fucked up. Then I work out how it happened, and why, in a brutal self-assessment.
2) **Accept:** I treat the failure for what it was. I remind myself that I'm human and fallible, and that mistakes in life are inevitable.
3) **Advance:** I push on by drawing lessons from the error. If possible, I'll then reframe my negative situation as a positive event. For example, *I've lost a work contract but I now have the opportunity to explore alternative projects in X, Y or Z.* Or, *I've upset a person I really care about, but I now know a lot more about how to communicate with them from now on.*

We all screw up, but viewing our mistakes as lessons will help us to grow stronger and smarter.

Meanwhile, it's possible to prepare for life's inevitable problems before they become too much of an issue by assessing our parallel existences. Planning in this way is really no different from training in the military. For example, everybody who signed up for the Royal Marines Commandos understood that their immediate future was likely to be filled with physical suffering and emotional discomfort. The only way to get through it was to be ready by living the right life.

⊕ THE LOOK FORWARD

Mentally step into your parallel life (or Life A) for a short period, and assess what changes could be brought to bear – but only work on one or two key areas at first. For example, imagine putting aside the money you would have otherwise spent on takeaway meals and drinks, and see how the saved cash mounts up over the course of a month. Then imagine what might happen over a year. Implementing wider lifestyle changes becomes much easier once you've witnessed improvements on a smaller scale.

CHAPTER 7
THE EMOTIONAL STOCKTAKE (INTERNAL)

When we think of a stocktake, what do we see? A team of super-market shelf-stackers counting tins of beans, most probably, or the internal audit of a multimillion-pound business with account-ants and clerks poring over screens of numbers and transactions. These processes, while boring, are important. They help a com-pany to keep track of everything, so their inflows and outflows can be accounted for, and if there are any holes in the budget, or if a problem with the inventory pops up, it's possible to acknowledge mistakes, find solutions and fix any issues.

This process works elsewhere, too, and I've learned it's possible for an individual to perform a psychological stocktake, something I like to do every morning once I've woken up. While the concept may sound weird, what's taking place is no different from the shelf-stacker counting tins of beans or the auditor scanning fig-ures and charts: I'm taking stock of what's gone into my person emotionally, what's gone out, and what's happened to me as a result. It only takes a few minutes, and in doing an inventory of this kind I'm able to gain a greater understanding of my mental state. I'll always take particular care of myself in this area when I've completed a mission, whether that's a period of time spent working away from home or a physical endeavour that might have taxed my body and brain.

A good example of how this process has benefited me would be my state of mind as a newly badged elite operator. In my early days on the job, I believed I was an imposter, even though I'd got the position on merit and was trained to an incredibly high standard. And yet every day I felt I was out of place, or out of my depth. I told myself that I didn't deserve to be there and that everyone else around me knew it. But after a period of emotional stocktaking, I realized my teammates felt the exact same way, because all of us had been locked into a constant phase of learning. *We all felt like imposters.* We had to, if we were to survive in a rapidly evolving environment where our adversaries hoped to kill us. In fact, the stress of falling behind was keeping us sharp. Conducting an emotional stocktake helped me to arrive at that conclusion and my imposter syndrome soon faded away.

Here's how emotional stocktaking works for me:

Step One: Every morning, without fail, I'll wake up, sit at the end of my bed and run an emotional stocktake. This is performed by asking one simple question:

'How am I feeling?'

Step Two: If I'm in good shape, I'll crack on with my day. If I'm feeling off, or if I'm unsure of what's going on emotionally, I'll dig a little deeper. It might be that I'm in a grumpy mood. If so, is that feeling a direct reaction to an event? Or is it symptomatic of some deeper issue, such as nerves, sadness or stress? With the cause established, I'll ask another question:

'What immediate steps can I take to fix the feeling?'

Step Three: If there's something I can do to resolve the issue, I'll crack on with it immediately. If I'm unable to ease the negativity, or if I'm struggling to acknowledge exactly what's going on, I'll tell myself:

'It's OK, the feeling of uncertainty will fade eventually.'

Weirdly, that simple act is sometimes enough to take the pressure off and helps to place me in a better state of mind. As a result I'm able to function more effectively and interact with the people around me, without coming across like a bear with a sore head.

TACTICAL BRIEFING: ACKNOWLEDGE THE 'WEIRD'

When running an emotional stocktake, it's not unusual for me to come up with a vague, intangible response. I can't quite put my finger on what's bugging me, but I know it's not good. In a nutshell, I feel . . . *weird*. Previously, that sensation used to bother me. I often became annoyed that I couldn't figure out exactly what was going on emotionally and it worried me that something was taking place that I didn't fully understand. But in the end I realized that feeling weird was an emotion in itself and usually a symptom of some other issue. I only had to run a deeper emotional audit to discover what that issue was.

This often happens to me when I get home after filming abroad for weeks, or even months, on end. I'll settle back into the familiar rhythms of home life with my partner, and on the surface everything seems cool, but in the background there's always an odd feeling – a sense that something's not quite right. It's nothing to do with my other half; it's more a nagging warning sign that I'm not at 100 per cent.

When it first started happening, I went quiet for long periods, or shut down, because I couldn't work out what was going on. I imagine that was pretty unsettling for my friends and family. But after a while, I came to view the sensation of feeling slightly off-balance as a process: it was my head's way of correcting an issue that I might not have been fully aware of in the moment, such as travel fatigue, frustration at something that went wrong during filming, or stress at how a certain situation might have looked on camera. I quickly learned that it was far better for me to acknowledge weirdness as a valid emotion than to ignore it. These days, I'll tell people around me what's happening and I'll lean into the uncertainty, trusting that the truth of what's really bothering me will come to the surface. From there I can act accordingly.

⊙ THE LOOK FORWARD

Make an emotional stocktake part of your day. The time at which you conduct yours isn't really important (I've built mine into my morning routine), but always take a few minutes to conduct one every twenty-four hours. Maybe you're feeling great – but if things seem off in any way, ask yourself some follow-up questions:

1) Is this emotion valid?
2) Is the situation that's causing this emotion within my control, or not?
3) If it's within my control, what steps can I take to rectify it?

CHAPTER 8
THE EMOTIONAL STOCKTAKE (EXTERNAL)

While businesses and supermarkets run stocktakes to assess the state of their finances or supply levels all the time, problems will mount up if any troubling results aren't communicated across the company. For example, if left unaddressed:

- Holes in the accounts might lead to long-term financial issues.
- Relevant changes to the inventory won't be made.
- Any teachable moments will be missed. In the case of a supermarket, this could be the items that regularly run out of stock at specific times, such as Christmas.

Any stocktake that glosses over a company's flaws is a massive waste of time. The same can be said of an emotional stocktake: it's no good running an internal audit and then bottling up the results. It's vital we share any negative results with the people around us so that our state of mind can be understood and won't cause conflicts. If ever I'm feeling off, for whatever reason, the first person I'll tell is my wife, but it can sometimes help to alert any friends and colleagues I might be spending time with.

I recently experienced this problem during filming of *SAS: Who Dares Wins*, when a few members of the camera crew seemed to be acting a little weirdly towards the Directing Staff (DS). Much of it was understandable: the show's production schedule definitely seemed more hectic than usual, due to several political issues that had kicked off. The resulting emotional blowback affected everyone's work and it was hard not to pick up on the tension, but because teammate Mark 'Billy' Billingham and I had been trained in an environment where hurt feelings counted for very little, we didn't pull any punches. We shot down any crap ideas in meetings (as we always did) but I sensed we were regarded as 'high-maintenance', even though we had been maintaining an elite professional standard. As filming came to a close, I felt paranoid and awkward.

In reality, both groups had been struggling in the high-pressure environment. I later learned that the crew had been under serious stress due to a combination of logistical and personal issues. Meanwhile, the DS had felt unbalanced because we were under constant surveillance, 24/7, for ten days and it had become more claustrophobic than usual. The cameras were never off us, even while we were getting dressed. At times I was naked and getting my kit ready, knowing that somebody was watching, which is a pretty vulnerable spot to be in.

Sadly, neither side addressed their problems with the other, and at the end of filming I had the feeling that some of the crew viewed the DS as prima donnas – and vice versa – when both groups were only trying to be professional.

What I've learned from that experience is that all of us should have conducted an internal emotional stocktake before sharing the results, externally. Certainly, if I'd known the crew were feeling beasted, I'd have taken on a more empathetic tone when working alongside them. Likewise, I'm sure that if the crew had understood the DS were only trying to maintain a level of high performance in certain areas, they would have been less critical. The mistake we all made was a lack of communication.

I mentioned this to the show's psychiatrist as we left for home. I said, 'Next time, when you have your time with the crew, just let them know where the DS are at. Likewise, we should be told if there are any problems behind the scenes, because how they interact with us has a big impact on our mindset. If we don't know there are other issues going on, their actions make us paranoid, we become jumpy and react badly, and that then becomes a vicious cycle.'

How I'll carry that idea into future projects remains to be seen, but I've learned a valuable lesson when performing an emotional stocktake: when it comes to moving forward positively in a team environment, intelligence-sharing is everything.

TACTICAL BRIEFING: MAXIMIZE YOUR SOLITUDE

I'm a people person. Most of the time I'll prefer company to a period of solitude, though I've learned to enjoy the quieter moments in life, probably because I'm rarely on my own. When life slows down, I'm usually listening to podcasts, watching documentaries or reading books. There's always some form of escapism. Rarely am I sitting on a sofa, staring off into space. However, whenever I am occasionally free of other people and distraction, I like to get a handle on what's going on in my head, because solitude is the best place in which to conduct an emotional stocktake.

A recent example of that took place on a work trip where I had to quarantine in a hotel for two weeks as part of the country's entry requirements. There was a sense of dread among the people I'd been travelling with. After a succession of lockdowns and pandemic stressors, they were understandably nervous about enduring yet another period of confinement. I wasn't exactly keen on the idea myself. But within a few days of being cooped up, I came to realize the benefits: I was free of work hassle; nobody was asking me to be here, there and everywhere, all at once; and I had plenty of space in which to check in with my emotions.

After my initial stocktake, I felt weird, and I couldn't put my finger on why. There was a chance it was jetlag, but over the first forty-eight hours it transpired that being detached from my friends, loved ones and a solid home routine had unbalanced me more than I thought it would. Luckily, identifying the root cause of my weirdness helped me to overcome it. I talked to people at home regularly, and as soon as I'd reconnected with the rest of my working group at the end of our quarantine period, I made sure to express how I'd felt, in case I was coming across as being stand-offish or distant.

→ THE LOOK FORWARD

If ever life feels a little off-kilter, practise mentioning it to anyone around you who might be affected by your weird mood. It could be a partner, a mate or a work colleague. You don't even have to explain the cause of your discomfort. Instead, just state that you're in a strange headspace and reassure them that any negative re-actions you might have aren't a result of their behaviour, but of how you're feeling.

CHAPTER 9
TAKE A BREATH

While I was serving in the military there was never any training in the area of breathwork, and I can remember hyperventilating a few times when life got noisy, so clearly I could have done with an education in its effects on the nervous system, especially during times of extreme stress. But since leaving military service, I've learned a lot about the use of tactical breathing and how it can help a person to recover from a variety of pressurized situations.

One element in this discovery process arrived after a chat I had with the hardcore Dutch athlete and sub-zero guru Wim Hof – the man made famous, through a string of TV shows, books and documentaries, for his ability to thrive in brutally cold temperatures. Wim has long preached the virtues of ice baths, cold showers and controlled breathing. If done correctly, Wim reckons this practice can work wonders for a person's stress, focus, sleep, determination and immune system,* and his technique generally involves the following six steps:

- **Step One:** Take a full, powerful breath in through your nostrils.
- **Step Two:** Exhale gently through your mouth.
- **Step Three:** Repeat thirty times.
- **Step Four:** After the thirtieth inhalation, empty your lungs by approximately 90 per cent and hold your breath for as long as you can.

* The scientific jury is still out on some of these theories.

- **Step Five:** Once you've maxed out, suck in another full lung-load of air and hold again for fifteen seconds.
- **Step Six:** Repeat Steps One to Five a total of three times.

My own personal experiences with breathwork have only ever really focused on calming the mind in times of chaos. Despite my mentioning hyperventilating once or twice on missions, I do recall situations where I'd sit in the back of a plane or helicopter before a parachute jump and gulp down a settling breath or three. Recently, on my speaking tour, I used breathing techniques to calm my butterflies by filling my lungs with a powerful inhalation before standing up fully and exhaling with a loud '*Aaaaaaaah!*' This helped to boost my confidence. I was also taught how to hold my breath effectively during a free-diving session, where there was an understandable tendency to panic once my lungs had been emptied underwater. The session taught me that I had at least two minutes before my body experienced the debilitating effects of oxygen deprivation, and I was soon able to push past the freak-out stage and function effectively at depth. This gave me more evidence that breathwork, like physical fitness and a calm mind, is a powerful resource when used tactically.

TACTICAL BRIEFING: THE OXYGEN ARMOURY

There are a number of breathing exercises and each of them can help the body to recover from different negative emotional states, whether that's stress, demotivation, fatigue, anxiety or anger. Learning just a handful will build an armoury of techniques for boosting the nervous system.

PROBLEM ONE: YOU'RE IN CHAOS – YOU FEEL FRAZZLED.

Solution: Box breathing.

How It Works and How to Do It: Breathe deeply into the lungs – this draws more oxygen into the body than during shallow breathing; it also expels more stale oxygen. The process helps reduce stress and increase concentration.

1) Slowly empty the lungs.
2) Inhale for four seconds – feel the oxygen in your belly.
3) Hold for four seconds.
4) Exhale for four seconds.
5) Repeat for as long as necessary.

PROBLEM TWO: YOU'RE ANXIOUS.

Solution: Alternate-nostril breathing.

How It Works and How to Do It: This process sets off the parasympathetic nervous system, which then helps to bring calm in times of stress. Some research also suggests that alternate nostril-breathing can increase a person's alertness.

1) Using your thumb, close your right nostril and inhale through your left.
2) Close the left nostril and exhale through your right.
3) With the left nostril still closed, inhale through your right.
4) To complete the cycle, close the right side, open the left, and exhale.
5) Do this for approximately five minutes, making sure to round things up by breathing out of your left nostril on your final breath.

PROBLEM THREE: YOU'RE WOUND UP.

Solution: Bumble-bee breathing.

How It Works and How to Do It: Bumble-bee breathing stimulates the vagus nerve in the brain, which in turn triggers the body's parasympathetic nervous system. This then lowers the user's heart rate and blood pressure, and helps to soothe the head.

1) Breathe in slowly.
2) As you exhale (again, slowly) hum like a bee.
   You might feel like a bell-end, but trust me on this one.
3) Repeat for as long as you want to.

PROBLEM FOUR: IT'S TIME TO SWITCH ON.

Solution: Bellows breathing.

How It Works and How to Do It: This breathing technique is known to ramp up alertness levels, sharpen our thinking and even fire up the body. It does this by stimulating the sympathetic nervous system, which is responsible for triggering our fight-or-flight response.

1) Close your mouth, but keep it relaxed. Don't clench.
2) Get the diaphragm moving by quickly breathing in and out of your nose in equal bursts. Go for three rounds of inhalations and exhalations, and then start breathing normally again.
3) Aim for ten reps per round. And take a break of twenty seconds between each round.

⊕ THE LOOK FORWARD

If you tend to breathe through your mouth at night, buy some mouth tape from your local chemist or online. (A box only costs a few quid.) Doing so will act as a health boost because breathing through the nose strengthens an individual's immune system (immunoglobulin is produced), reduces the amount of allergen particles entering the body (thanks to the filtering effects of the nasal passages) and improves oxygen absorption (because breathing through the nose produces nitric oxide, which helps with this process). Sealing the mouth might feel weird at first, but you'll soon get used to it.

(Safety advice: Do not attempt this style of breathing if you have a full stomach, a heart condition, high blood pressure, hypertension, you're pregnant, if you suffer from panic-related conditions, migraines or seizures, or if you've recently undergone abdominal surgery. *If in doubt, check with your doctor.*)

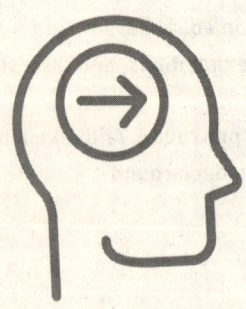

CHAPTER 10
IF THERE'S FUCK ALL TO DO, DO FUCK ALL

In a war zone there's little hope of grabbing the doctor-prescribed eight hours of kip. Conflict doesn't exactly run to a civilized schedule, and while working as an elite operator there were plenty of occasions when I had to work while feeling exhausted. That wasn't a problem back then – I was younger, keener, and I'd been trained in such a way that it was possible to function with limited rest, though there was a definite drop-off in sharpness if I'd been rolling in and out of raids for days on end. That said, I was still able to nail my work effectively when I was feeling knackered, even after kipping beneath a helicopter in the desert for only an hour or so. However, when rested, my mood was solid, there was a noticeable uptick in my performance levels and I felt enthusiastic.

These days I'm different. I try to grab my eight hours as much as possible, and for good reason: being rested is a major boost for memory, concentration, performance, immunity from illness and infection, mood and tactical decision-making. (*No shit*.) I've even built a night-time routine that's every bit as important as my morning one. (See Part Four, Chapter 2.) Meanwhile, serving at the military's sharpest point has taught me two valuable lessons:

IF YOU CAN'T GET A GOOD NIGHT'S SLEEP, DON'T STRESS.

Since turning my emotional state around, I've built a positive set of routines and systems to keep my mental health in check, but if ever a situation prevents me from resting fully, or taking the cold shower that I like first thing in the morning, I won't stress that it might affect my performance levels. Instead, I'll remember back to the times when I lived off catnaps for days on end while surviving in some of the harshest environments on Earth. I know that while the recovery components of my routine are important, they're not always essential for success. I can get by.

IF THERE'S FUCK ALL TO DO, DO FUCK ALL.

Get in the sleeping bag. This was a concept that was often pushed on to us in the military, because burnout was a very real concern. Whenever weather or helicopter issues grounded us, the top brass usually ordered us to rest. For the most part, we sat around and watched films, messed about or trained in the gym. Though I was always petrified of overdoing it in case we had to yomp 10km to target during our next operation. It helped to lift our energy levels a bit.

This idea was first drummed into me during the Marines. When there was work to be done, we had to do it quickly and effectively, but in times of inactivity, we were taught that recovery was vital if we were to function to the best of our abilities once life became hectic again. There was no point burning mental or physical calories executing tasks unless they were going to help me mentally, physically or tactically.

Sadly this concept hasn't crossed over to the civilian world, where too many organizations have become fixated with gluing their staff to a desk, even when the velocity of work has temporarily slowed down. I know this from experience. For a brief while after leaving the military I took a job in the corporate world. As team leader of a small department it was my role to look after three auditors and a secretary. One day I noticed everybody sitting at their workstations. They looked bored out of their brains.

'What are you doing?' I said.

'Oh, we're working,' came the response.

'No, you're not. There's fuck all to do. So, if you've done your work, just sod off home.'

The team couldn't believe it. This wasn't a process they were familiar with, but I knew they would return the next day feeling refreshed and more eager to work. The accounts manager, when he found out, seemed equally confused by my decision, and just a little bit annoyed.

'They're still getting paid – you can't send them home!' he moaned. 'Find them something to do next time.'

'Like *what*?' I said. 'This lot are on the ball. They've got nothing outstanding and my hunch is that they'll be more productive in the morning.'

I knew all too well the dangers of exerting needless effort in a team situation. When working for working's sake, boredom usually kicks in, morale drops, and the group becomes fatigued and demotivated shortly afterwards. What's needed is a break – some downtime, a team-bonding event or a change of pace such as a training exercise or a period of active recovery. Apply this tactic to your own routines. If there's nothing for you or your team to do, put your feet up and recover in a productive way. And make sure to avoid FOMO or the sense of guilt that can accompany a period of inactivity. Tell yourself you'll soon be needed at full strength. There's bound to be some battle on the way and it's important you prepare accordingly.

Then get in the sleeping bag.

TACTICAL BRIEFING: THE DANGER OF OVERWORKING

If you need any further evidence as to why you should take time to rest then consider the fact that being knackered is actually as bad for you in performance terms as being over the alcohol limit when driving. In a 1997 study entitled *Fatigue, Alcohol and Performance Impairment*, the researchers, Drew Dawson and Kathryn Reid, discovered that reduced sleep can impact a person's so-called 'cognitive psychomotor performance' by a significant amount: within the forty-person sample pool, it was recorded that individuals lost 0.74 per cent of performance levels every hour after they had been awake for ten hours.

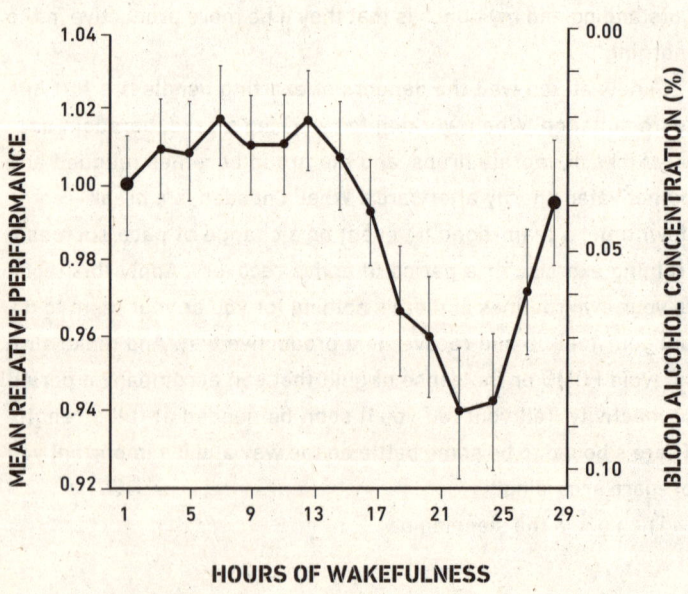

Dawson and Reid eventually concluded that after seventeen hours of wakefulness, the performance levels in a person were similar to someone who had a 0.05% blood-alcohol concentration. 'This is the proscribed level of alcohol intoxication in many western industrialized countries,' they said. More worryingly, after twenty-four hours, this number rose to 0.10 per cent, which I found terrifying. Remember, for much of my career I was jumping out of planes and chasing down bad dudes on zero kip.

⊕ THE LOOK FORWARD

Master the art of dropping off. If you're struggling, use this five-step technique that has long been taught by the US military. In tests, personnel trained in this method were able to fall asleep in less than two minutes.

1) Get comfy.
2) Relax your face. No frowning, no clenching.
3) Let your shoulders go heavy . . .
4) . . . and then your legs.
5) Switch off your brain by thinking of a peaceful scene such as a seaside sunset.

You should be asleep in no time. Mastering this process takes around six weeks, but it was successful in 96 per cent of participants in the first tests.

CHAPTER 11
ELIMINATE TOXICITY

All of us have a certain element of toxicity in our lives, whether we know it or not. It might be that an unhealthy romantic relationship has placed us into an emotionally bad place. We've all had that mate who lands us in trouble after a skinful. In the workplace, a toxic presence could be undermining our efforts or the productivity of the whole team. In some cases our entire environment could be regarded as toxic, and our home, work and social lives could all be threatening to unhinge us from a healthy way of living. Thankfully, there's a fairly basic technique for extracting ourselves from these situations – but it isn't easy.

Get rid. *And fast*.

I know it's a difficult process, because I've been there on several occasions. Some of my ex-girlfriends have been bad for me. They've tried to exert an unnecessary amount of control over my life, or acted in a manipulative way that then impacted upon my mental health. I've had friends that could be considered wildcards, particularly in the way they've behaved, and their actions have caused conflict. When I left the military I even had a job that was toxic for my well-being. In this case it was definitely me and not them: I didn't have any real structure in my life, so I didn't know whether I was coming or going half the time, and the role required me to drive around the country for hours on end. In a desperate attempt to work out, I'd squeeze in training sessions on random football pitches or in parks I passed in the car, but the process, while making the best of a bad situation, was unrewarding most of the time. I felt like my life was falling apart.

Once I'd acknowledged the damage these situations were causing, I cut them away. The same thing happened with my relationship with alcohol. While I wouldn't describe my drinking as dangerous or overly negative, it can soften my edges a little. I put on weight – I don't look fat, but it's easy to tell that I'm heavier; I don't feel as good as when I'm lighter, quicker and sharper in the gym. I'm also not as productive as when I'm clear of booze; my work isn't squared away as effectively as I'd like. So, every now and then, I'll stop drinking. I don't announce it or make a big proclamation – *'That's it! Me and beer are done.'* Instead, I tell myself I'm taking a break and I can go back to it when I feel ready. My discipline in this area has been solid.

This attitude may sound ruthless, but that's because I've been shown first-hand how the military deals with toxic people and processes, and it involves zero fucking about. If the top brass ever recognized a disruptive individual within our ranks, they binned them off immediately. (The same attitude was also applied to redundant tactical manoeuvres, training procedures or even technology.) At the top tier, the hierarchy analysed the performances of their assets. If one person was found to be causing serious division or disruption within the group, they were dispatched back to their regular unit. This robust system meant that it was on the individual to hold themselves and their performances accountable. If they didn't, someone higher up would do the job for them, and their negative performance results were used as evidence to end any debate in the matter. The alternative was to leave a toxic presence in a highly trained and valuable unit, where it would spread like a cancer before bringing the group down.

TACTICAL BRIEFING: LOCATE YOUR WEAK SPOT

Some of us have a toxicity in our lives that's fairly easy to spot because it clearly prevents us from performing to the best of our abilities. Examples might include:

- **An unhealthy relationship with a substance or activity, such as booze or gambling.**
- **The friend that drags us into conflict.**
- **The partner that brings us down.**

In these cases, it's important we ask one question before pressing the ejector-seat button: can the situation be improved?

- **In the case of a negative activity, could we establish a healthy level of usage?**
- **Is it possible to set boundaries with our wildcard mate?**
- **Can my relationship issues be solved with better communication or counselling?**

If the answer is 'no': you know what to do. Of course, there will always be self-deception – the part of us that denies there's even a problem in the first place:

- **My gambling or drinking isn't *that* big a problem.**
- **He/she is actually OK. They won't do it again.**
- **We'll get over the hump – our relationship will definitely improve with time.**

Sure, in some cases these proclamations may be true – I'm not asking you to act without thought. Only you'll know, though. The answer will be deep down in your gut. You just have to act on it as quickly as possible, and making that decision requires discipline. However, the consequences of not doing it are clear: avoiding the problem will only allow it to spread. Take it from someone that has cut away negative relationships, jobs, friends and habits: it isn't easy – it's not supposed to be – but the exercise will reduce the conflict in your life while improving your health and happiness levels in the long run.

⊕ THE LOOK FORWARD

Take some time to locate the toxicity in your life. Analyse the things that might be stopping you from hitting your full potential. It might be that you have a weekly drinking session with mates – the following day you feel like shit, eat badly and your performance levels drop as a result. Think about how you might improve that situation. Could you cut back on the alcohol intake? Or maybe make the sessions fortnightly, or even once a month, rather than every week? Sampling a better life beyond toxicity can sometimes act as a powerful motivator, so if you're unsure, give it a go and pay close attention to your energy and performance levels the next day.

CHAPTER 12
RESPECT THE PAIN

Getting injured is a headfuck. Not only because of the pain and frustration it can cause in the aftermath, but because it can also mess with our emotions, especially if the injury in question prevents us from doing something we really enjoy, or seriously interferes with our routine in a debilitating way. Luckily, I was never seriously hurt during my time in the military – well, apart from one or two bumps and cuts, and a niggly knee that kept me out of one mission; I also got stung by a scorpion in the jungle during my first Selection and had to medically withdraw when the wound became infected. But it could have been so much worse. I've seen lads have their lives permanently altered by a round or an IED blast. The emotional destruction that is inflicted during those events can be just as crushing as the physical.

One of the most serious injuries I've experienced happened quite recently, when I was filming the American version of *SAS: Who Dares Wins*, a show called *Special Forces: World's Toughest Test*. It was my job to demonstrate an abseil down the side of a 300-foot-tall control tower for the watching celebrity recruits. I'd previously conducted one or two test runs and everything had gone well. But when the cameras rolled for the first time, I was around 100 feet from the floor when I realized my descent was too fast. I looked below me: a ledge that was built into the bottom of the tower was rearing up at me. On previous runs I'd dropped clean past it, but this time, for some unknown reason, I was on a collision course.

As I stuck out my leg to kick away, I felt something pop in my ankle.

Having landed, there wasn't any pain. My initial thought was that I might have sprained something, and I felt weird, maybe a little bit sick. Then my teammate Mark 'Billy' Billingham came over to check on me. When I tried to stand, my whole leg seemed to buckle. Something was off, but still I tried to convince myself that there wasn't a problem. *I really didn't want to be injured*.

'It'll be alright,' I said. 'I'll walk it off.'

But when the doctor came to check me over, I was told there was no way I was walking anything off. I had likely broken both my fibula and tibia in two places. As I was sped through the desert by some mad driver to a local military hospital, the only thing keeping the pain away was the happy gas. When the injury was confirmed I felt gutted. I was screwed, and staring down the barrel of a lengthy recovery process. Worse, I was then ordered to wear a plastic boot that made me look like a right dick.

TACTICAL BRIEFING: LEAN INTO THE INJURY VORTEX

All sorts of emotions can kick up after an injury. Depression. Loneliness. Frustration. Demotivation. Rage. There can be physical reactions as a result, too, including disrupted sleep patterns, fatigue and major nutritional changes, such as over- or under-eating. Rarely does someone emerge from an injury feeling psychologically better, especially if the inciting incident was traumatic in some way, such as a car crash or a horror tackle on the rugby pitch.

Every emotional response is different, though, and there is no set path to negotiating the feelings that can arise following a painful setback, other than to acknowledge the emotions and deal with them accordingly. I know from the experience of breaking my leg that the mental process I had to endure mirrored that of the five stages of grief: denial, anger, bargaining, depression and, finally, acceptance.

DENIAL

When grieving death or the break-up of a relationship, it's easy to deny that anything is happening at all. A lot of people will tell themselves that they're OK, or that the split from their significant other will be fixed in no time at all. But this is a coping mechanism that helps us deal with what is an overwhelming rush of emotions. Similarly, in the moments after screwing up my abseil, I told myself it was nothing: I was fine. *I can walk it off.* That was a load of bollocks, though, and deep down I knew it.

ANGER

When grieving, we beat ourselves up for anything we might have said and done to the person we've lost, or we lash out at others. The good news is that anger is a sign that our pain is being expressed, but it's also the one emotion I try to get a kibosh on because I know how destructive it can be – to both the people around me and myself. There are physiological reasons for managing anger, too. An Ohio State University study once gave blisters to ninety-eight people as part of an experiment. After several days it was found the subjects with anger-management issues had healed more slowly than those without. Following my injury, there were moments when I could have gone off at someone. I was definitely moody for a while, but if ever I felt my anger rising, I worked through it productively by exercising (albeit in a limited way) or taking some time out for myself.

BARGAINING

This is the moment in a break-up when one person makes a promise to the other that they'll 'change' as an attempt to heal the rift. In my case, bargaining took on the shape of treatments and supplements. I wore compression socks. I met with physios. I took magnesium supplements. I even tried powdered collagen in my drinks. Some of these remedies may have worked, some of them may have been placebos, but all of them were my way of bartering with the healing process in the hope that I might recover more quickly than the doctors had suggested.

DEPRESSION

While there were moments where I became very down about my situation, I didn't get depressed for long periods, as some people can. Instead I felt frustrated at my inability to do the things that I loved, like working out or prepping for the next season of *SAS: Who Dares Wins*. One thing I do remember is that I felt moody whenever certain decisions were placed into the hands of others. For instance, the producers of the show wanted to know if I could do a recce trip for a forthcoming series – the work was going to take me into the jungle. But my surgeon and physio explained to the producers that I wasn't ready. That brought me down a bit, I think because it reminded me of that time in my military career when a scorpion sting had forced me to medically withdraw from my first Selection. Back then I'd sulked in my hospital bed for days, wondering if I'd ever pass the entry course to the UK Armed Forces' top tier. My setback felt like a dream-shattering event, when in reality it was nothing of the sort.

ACCEPTANCE

This was arguably the most painful stage in the process for me, but it also represented a breakthrough: I realized I'd done myself in and that my leg needed to take some time to heal properly. But after a while of acknowledging the painful reality of the situation, my mood lifted. I understood what I needed to do if I was to recover fully. And with a rehab plan in place, I felt a sense of hope that I could reach peak fitness once more.

→ THE LOOK FORWARD

If you've experienced an injury or illness, take some time to sit with the feelings you're experiencing and act accordingly.

TALK IT OUT

It might be that you were injured by the actions of another person and there's some residual anger. Find someone who you can talk to about the pain, like a friend or therapist. If the feeling still lingers after you've healed, maybe try some outlets for your frustration – boxing and martial arts are always good, or practice breathwork.

STAY IN CONTACT

Maybe you're part of a team or club and your injury is preventing you from competing alongside your mates. Make sure you still mix with the brother- or sisterhood. Go to the games. Support the team. Attend the socials. You'll find they'll make for a great support group. Their successes and failures will inspire you to stick to your recovery.

RE-EVALUATE

If your injury has shattered your short- or medium-term plans in some way, then make new ones. I know from personal experience that there's no better time in which to establish a new target than when you're flat on your back in a protective boot.

CHAPTER 13
REBUILD FROM THE BRAIN

After breaking my leg in 2022, I spent a bit of time moping about the house like a bear with a sore arse, as a lot of people do during the anger phase of an injury. My temperament wasn't even improved by the prospect of a restorative holiday abroad. That had a lot to do with the fact that I was travelling to a nice resort in a supportive boot and compression socks, my suitcase weighed down with a warehouse-load of supplements and vitamins, all so that I could heal more quickly. At first I tried to do some limited training in the resort gym, but my leg hurt like hell and I was spun out by the realization I would have to fully rest up again, only able to move around the resort in a plastic welly, like RoboCop.

'This is shit,' I moaned one morning. 'It's not supposed to feel like this.'

I went into a negative spiral. My low emotional state reminded me of a holiday I'd shared with an ex. At that time I'd known my head was a mess: I was leaving the military elite, so there was a fear that my identity might be going with it. It didn't help that Osama bin Laden was killed while I was sitting on the beach, and I felt as if I'd missed out on the culmination of years of military service. So when I injured my leg in 2022, I became a terrible person to be around because my latest bad mood reminded me of one from my past. That amplified my frustration even more. In the end, I forced myself to snap out of it.

'You've got to shift this state of mind,' I told myself, with a reminder I'd been trained by the Royal Marines to think that cheerfulness in the face of adversity was the best way of unfucking a fucked-up situation.

I worked on quickly thinking positively by digging into all the ways I could speed up my recovery time, and I realized that just because I couldn't work on myself physically (other than through some of the rehabilitation exercises I'd been prescribed), there was nothing to stop me from working on myself psychologically, so I dug into the science. It turned out that a number of studies had proved it was possible for an individual to grow in strength through visualization, the most famous example being a 2004 paper by the exercise psychologist Guang Yue, entitled *From Mental Power to Muscle Power – Gaining Strength by Using the Mind*, which examined the efforts of athletes working on their finger abduction strength. Those who trained physically saw their power increase by 53 per cent; those who 'exercised' mentally still increased their capability by 35 per cent.

Rather than sitting around and feeling sorry for myself, I imagined myself walking freely, without a clunky boot strapped to my peg, free of pain. I visualized treks through the woods, runs over hills with mates and lung-busting hikes across the Brecon Beacons. All I had to do was shut my eyes and picture the scene, and I was mentally back to my old self. After a while, I upped the stakes and imagined myself running over difficult terrain. In my head I felt strong: my legs were moving like pistons and every movement felt light and easy. Whether this had a direct impact on my recovery, it's hard to say, but my rehabilitation certainly felt a lot easier than it had done when I'd spent my time sulking.

I then remembered the All Blacks rugby star Sonny Bill Williams, who suffered a ruptured Achilles tendon while competing in the 2016 Olympics. Rather than letting the injury derail his fitness, Sonny sat at his stationary rower, his injured leg lying straight on a skateboard, and thrashed away like a beast. Struck with inspiration, I later repeated the technique in the gym, moving my protective boot along on the board while I rowed at speed. And while it might not have been the perfect workout, it was better than nothing. Meanwhile, the effort also delivered an important lesson: visualization had encouraged me to improvise and that meant I could maintain my endurance levels.

TACTICAL BRIEFING: POSITIVE HEALING

There's an obvious reason why the Royal Marines preach the concept of cheerfulness in the face of adversity to every recruit that crawls across the muddy training field in the pissing rain and freezing cold: in tough times positivity acts as fuel, whereas a negative mindset can spread like a cancer and debilitate a unit of people faced with a daunting task. But the concept also works for a person's well-being. A 2017 study on the emotional perspective of people suffering from potentially fatal conditions discovered that optimism, or a lack of it, can have a massive impact on whether they will recover fully, or not.

The researchers, from the University of Essex, Curtin University in Australia and Jyväskylä University in Finland, discovered that there was a direct correlation between the people who thought positively about their recovery and those who overcame their illness. Meanwhile, those who allowed themselves to be overwhelmed by negative emotion were more likely to struggle when tackling their illness, and their treatments.

'This study examined the science of illness beliefs and their effects on how people with chronic illnesses, such as cancer, diabetes and cardiovascular disease, cope with their illness and whether they will recover or live with their illness effectively,' said Professor Martin Hagger of Curtin University. 'The study found people who view their illness as more serious and symptomatic, and have strong negative emotions about it, were more likely to adopt avoidance or go into denial to cope. Those people are also more likely to experience depression and anxiety, and they are less likely to get better.'

⊖ THE LOOK FORWARD

When working through an injury – either a physical or emotional one – or illness, spend some time visualizing how you'll be after you've recovered. If you've wrenched your back in an accident, picture yourself moving freely as you exercise, or playing your favourite sport. Use the positive feelings that come with being free of pain as inspiration when the rehabilitation gets really tough. And remember Guang Yue's research: it is possible to think yourself stronger.

PART THREE:
CHAOS

INTRODUCTION

For large chunks of my life, I've lived in extreme chaos. During my military career, I was exposed to the type of working environments that most people would consider unmanageable – jungles, deserts, mountains, and more. Meanwhile, war was hell, and I witnessed death and destruction at an alarming frequency. For that reason, my default psychological setting was often survival because I operated in situations where my ending was a very real possibility. And yet I thrived because I'd been trained in such a way that none of those issues felt debilitating.

Though these experiences were undoubtedly extreme, the emotions I felt within them can be regarded as familiar because chaos is chaos, and we all go through it at various points in our lives. On the low level, simply commuting to work can create a stressful background chatter; then there are the daily issues of finances, work, health and relationships. Sure, these factors might not create a chaotic situation all by themselves, but when combined they can potentially cause us to crack.

Then there are those issues that can strike us out of nowhere. Bereavement and personal tragedy; serious injury or illness; the break-up with a significant other or divorce. We might lose our job, experience a horrendous stroke of bad luck, like a house fire, or become embroiled in some geo-political situation. (You only have to look at Ukraine to see how normality can be upturned in a heartbeat.) Like everyone, I've experienced chaotic life experiences such as death, illnesses in loved ones, and divorce. And all of them felt terrible in the moment. Some of the less obvious issues, such as family or work-related stresses, were often hard to recognise

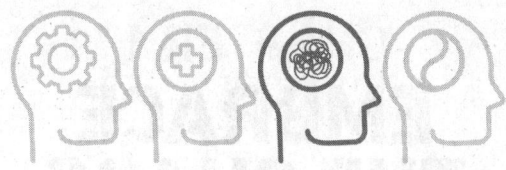

as being chaotic at first. Luckily, because of my training I was able to stay calm as the drama unfolded around me.

Currently I live a life that many people would still consider to be overly dangerous and chaotic. I've interviewed hitmen and drug-cartel leaders. I've visited war zones and violent no-go areas in lawless countries. I've crossed canyons on high wires, abseiled down buildings and cliff faces, and fast-roped from helicopters on to rapidly moving ships. In an attempt to push through my comfort zone, I rowed across the Atlantic and paddled down the Yukon. None of these endeavours have been easy and the mortal risk attached to all of them was high, but I survived because I knew how to thrive in chaos, thanks to a handful of processes instilled in me during military training, plus the emotional tools that were developed as I healed from my mental-health issues. I'll now share these techniques so that you can use them to steer yourself through any future pockets of emotional turbulence.

CHAPTER 1
EMBRACE THE CHAOS

As individuals, we're unable to prevent life's more destabilizing events; unexpected deaths, natural disasters, financial collapses and political upheavals are just a few of the challenges that can impact a person, and any one of them will create a shedload of negative emotion. *That's not good.* In times of crisis, our feelings will sometimes turn against us and if an individual allows grief, fear or shame to overwhelm them, there's every chance they'll wilt and fail in the scrap. Over the years, I've found that the best tactic for dealing with chaos is to square up to it with rational thought, because if you can face your situation calmly and logically, you'll likely swerve any avoidable associated traumas.

This attitude was introduced to me throughout military service, where we were constantly reminded to 'control the controllables' during chaotic situations where the stress was high. When the shooting started, or a mortar attack came out of nowhere, there was little point in me worrying about who was firing at us (the enemy was the enemy), or the exact number of hostiles we were dealing with. Those details were beyond my influence. Rather, my first step in gaining control was always to embrace the chaos by focusing my attentions on the variables I had power over. Whenever an ambush kicked off, my first instinct was to find the nearest point of cover. Once safely shielded, I conducted a head check on the lads, assessed any injured parties and then radioed back to base to alert them of our situation. From there, the team would figure out our next steps – for example, *Do we engage with the enemy now, or should we wait for air support?* Worrying about whether we were going to be overrun, or how long the gunfight might go on for, was a waste of mental calories.

Old habits can die hard and I adopted a similar attitude during the first weeks of the Covid-19 pandemic. At the time, a lot of people were understandably freaking out about the implications of a lockdown and what was a potentially deadly novel virus. But rather than embracing the chaos and using rational thought to plan their next steps, they allowed emotion to lead the way. Within days, the media was full of stories of people buying up *all* the loo roll, *all* the bottled water and *all* the hand sanitizer, as if the end of the world was taking place. People were acting irrationally and, as a consequence, the nation's supermarkets experienced serious stock shortages. Those who were genuinely in need of vital items, such as medical supplies, were sometimes unable to get them.

Don't get me wrong: the early outbreak of the pandemic was undoubtedly worrying. But experience had taught me that the best way of managing the chaos was to take cover and plan.

Right, I can live in this, I thought, *so there's no point spending shit-loads on bog roll or hand sanitizer. If the worst comes to the worst and I run out, I'll take a shower after the toilet and wash my hands with the soap we have.*

At the time, this was an appropriate response. My actions weren't worsening an already grim situation; I wasn't causing a headache for anyone else, either. More importantly, by ignoring the fear, leaning into common sense and gaining a little control, the chaos unfolding around me seemed less daunting. That meant I was more comfortable when planning my next move.

TACTICAL BRIEFING: THE USE OF COMMON-SENSE SYSTEMS

Navigating chaos is a challenge, but a manageable one. If we can put a system in place to ensure that we're able to function to the best of our ability during times of extreme stress, then we'll have a fairly good chance of making it to the other side unscathed. This theory is best illustrated by my response to the early stages of the pandemic. Having gained a little psychological control in a troubling situation, I assessed the factors within my influence. By the looks of things, personal hygiene was a major component when staying safe, so I set up a 'sanitation station' at home. I positioned bin liners, household cleaners and hand sanitizers by my front door and followed a simple routine whenever I came home from a walk:

1) Enter building. Sanitize hands at front door.
2) Strip off. Place clothes in bin liner. Sanitize hands again.
3) Spray bin liner with antibacterial cleaner, transfer to washing machine and load.
4) Shower.

With a solid system in place, I was able to prevent the potential spread of a then unknown and infectious virus. That allowed me to take further steps to protect my physical and mental health.

Each chaotic event is different and so I can't prescribe a catch-all system for dealing with every single one, though the one tactic I recommend you adopt is to root your first step in common sense. So, for example, it might be that you've lost a person very close to you, in which case you might want to implement a system of self-care whereby you eat clean, exercise frequently and cut down on your alcohol intake. This will allow you to mourn healthily and maintain greater control over your emotional state. Or maybe you've lost your job in a round of redundancies. Rather than ranting and raving for days on end about the injustices of it all, assess your financial position, set out a budget and explore where you can save money as you seek new employment. Ringing around for work in a desperate panic won't make you an attractive proposition to any potential employers. Instead, stay calm and ride out the storm.

⊖ THE LOOK FORWARD

When next faced with a moment of chaos, take cover and plan your next move. If you're hit with a terrifying bill and you're unable to pay, take stock of how you can either raise the money at a pinch, or improve your long-term financial situation. That way you won't be shocked again. This is easier said than done, I know, but just adding a free budgeting app to your phone and running a brutally honest assessment of what you spend can give you a clearer picture of your habits and monetary issues.

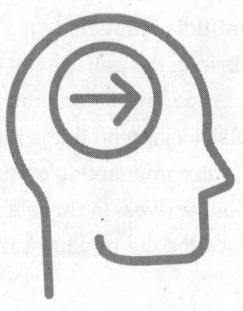

CHAPTER 2
THE TEN-SECOND RULE

Reacting too quickly in a chaotic situation is a dumb strategy, especially when sod-all thought is given to the consequences. I've lost count of the recruits on *SAS: Who Dares Wins* who have compounded an already precarious position by acting on kneejerk impulse. I've watched individuals bulldoze ahead during team time trials without checking their map properly; their rashness then leads their group into trouble. Or there's the classic hero type who tries to do it all and then becomes physically or mentally beasted at the worst possible moment, causing the rest of their team to fail too. Had those participants taken a very short amount of time to 1) breathe and 2) assess the situation before executing their chosen strategy, the outcomes might have been very different. Trust me: the process only takes ten seconds.

While this may not sound like a huge amount on the clock, a lot can still happen in that time, especially if you're stuck in a gunfight.* I know that the briefest of pauses can give a person enough wriggle room to gain perspective on an otherwise hectic situation. It might be someone else kicking off in the middle of a volatile dispute, a pressurized boardroom meeting or at home when an unexpectedly huge energy bill arrives. In those scenarios, ten seconds can create enough space for the mind to calm any overwhelming

---

* *If you don't believe me, the next time someone asks you a question, pause for ten seconds before answering. The wait will feel like an eternity.*

negative emotions, the situation can be viewed from a different angle, and within that space another person's perspective might become clearer. By adopting this tactic, it's possible for an individual to take control of the event, rather than allowing the event to exert control over them.

I recently put this theory into practice, having learned that somebody I was once close to was spreading malicious gossip about me online. They were even talking about going to the papers. I felt angry. I wanted to rant down the phone at the person in question. Then I remembered my military training: sure, yelling at the person might make me feel a little better, but not for long. Instead, I had to behave like the thinking soldier. In the end, I took ten seconds to breathe as I assessed my next move. I decided my first step should be to shift my perspective on the situation, and to do so I considered the position of the other people involved – the former friend and the newspaper editor – and checked in with myself again:

'Mate, what's the worst that can happen?'

Some gossip will appear in the papers.

'So what? Does it really matter?'

Not really, it's a nothing story that people will probably forget by lunchtime.

'So why is my former mate selling the story?'

To make a few quid, by the looks of it.

'How will that affect that person in the long run?'

They're going to look vindictive and desperate. If that's the case, then so be it. Roll with the punches and move on.

My frustration dissipated. I became calmer. Which was lucky because the alternative would have been to kick off and possibly worsen the situation. Sadly, I knew all too well the consequences of such a move. When I was around the age of twenty-one, I got into a scrap outside a nightclub. At that time I was inexperienced, naive and unable to control my emotions in a productive way. On this particular night, I'd taken a bit of abuse off a couple of lads and, rather than walking away or taking a few punches and ducking out of the conflict, I fought back. When the police showed up I was arrested and very nearly slung into prison. My military career looked to be over before I'd even fired a round in combat.

Anger is a funny emotion. I've often found myself in situations where I've applied the ten-second rule to an escalating confrontation and decided to walk away. But even though it was very much the right decision, I've sometimes become annoyed with myself afterwards. *Have I just been a fucking coward? Or have I saved myself a whole load of trouble?* Remembering the time my anger so nearly put me into prison reassures me that extracting myself is usually the best decision. Sadly, though, there are plenty of people who fail to slow themselves down in times of crisis. Road-rage drivers are a classic example: they can either look stupid (the best-case scenario) or inflict serious violence upon another person (the worst case). Certain blokes at the football (it's always the blokes) get so riled that they behave in a way that comes across as shocking to the fans around them. Gulping in a deep breath before lashing out would save those people a whole world of pain. It may be only ten seconds, but as a psychological tool in times of chaos, it can be enough to change the game.

TACTICAL BRIEFING: INACTIVITY IS A WEAPON

Slowing a situation down is one of the most important tools in the top tiers of military service. Very often, an enemy force will detonate an IED, or take pot-shots at an individual operator, in an attempt to manoeuvre the whole group into a trap. Once the group is snared, the hostile party can inflict greater damage and larger casualties. But in those situations, I found that the most effective tactic, if possible, was to order everyone into cover . . . *and do nothing*. We'd crouch down and wait, assessing the situation while ensuring that a fast-moving event didn't get beyond our control. This process also gave the enemy a fat middle finger – it sent out a message that stated: *We know what you're up to, but we're not falling for it*. After that, our response was always rapid and dynamic.

The same thing has happened when I've been filming *SAS: Who Dares Wins*. To the viewer, it might seem as if everything is running at a million miles per hour; that the action is relentless and everybody is moving at full speed, twenty-four hours a day. In reality, there are lulls in the action as the camera crew moves into a new position. In that time, the recruits are left to hang around, usually in the freezing cold or stifling heat. Meanwhile, the Directing Staff (DS) will usually take the opportunity to regroup. At first, those dead minutes used to freak me out. I didn't like the waiting. Then I realized that the inactivity was a resource I could draw upon in two ways:

I COULD TAKE A BREATHER AND FIGURE OUT
WHAT TO SAY NEXT

Delivering a powerful briefing to the recruits is tricky, especially if I've just spent ten minutes sprinting through a jungle. To negate the problem, I'll often stand around for a few minutes to compose myself beforehand. I might shout out a line or two that I know will look great for the editors, but if I become stuck for something else to say, I'll take a break to think. Once I've got everything figured out, I'll go again.

I COULD UNSETTLE THE RECRUITS

Silence is intimidating under the right circumstances. If you don't believe me, think of a time when you've cracked a joke and nobody has laughed, or made a comment in a meeting and it's been ignored. That kind of 'dead air' can freak a person out, but TV has made me realize it's possible to use this emotional discomfort as a weapon. I can remember incidents when the recruits have been gathering outside in the drill square or arriving at a new location. After lining them up in rows, I've told them to shut up and wait.

And then I'd do . . . *nothing*.

The silence was always powerful – and useful. From my viewpoint it was possible to get a greater understanding of who was coping with the challenge as a whole and who was buckling under the strain. I'd think: *I love this. I can do whatever I want* . . . And then, after a short period of time – maybe two minutes, maybe five – with the recruits overthinking the horribleness of their immediate future, I'd launch into the next briefing, knowing that I've impacted maximum psychological damage by doing absolutely nothing.

⊕ THE LOOK FORWARD

Practise slowing down a situation. The next time a negative statement is aimed your way, or some bad news is delivered, take a deep breath and wait ten seconds before acting. By acknowledging your feelings and becoming a calmer version of yourself, you stand a much better chance of responding in a positive way. If you don't have a chaotic situation in which to practise, make a point of reducing your walking speed in a crowded city centre or train station. Watch the frenzied movements of others. Certain people seem to storm around in a bad mood all day; they're almost waiting for a confrontation, having been enraged by an event they couldn't manage. By briefly slowing down, you'll come to understand the chaos around you and catch the warning signs way ahead of time, almost in slow motion, like Neo from *The Matrix*.

CHAPTER 3
DYNAMIC MEDITATION

Meditation is a great way to calm the mind in times of intense stress, but it usually requires a window of stillness and quiet. In times of chaos, those moments tend not to arrive. Even taking a ten-minute walk to calm the head can be a shitshow – there are all sorts of obstacles to keep an eye out for, like cars on the road, people cutting across your path, or a nasty change in the weather. At times it can feel like the only way to get a bit of peace is to stand in the corner of a library and mumble 'Mmmmmm . . .' over and over. Not that I'd recommend it: there's a good chance you'll get kicked out if you give it go.

When life gets noisy and I'm running about from place to place, I try to practise what I call 'dynamic meditation'. This is a variation on the traditional form, which takes place in moments of stillness. Rather than sitting in a peaceful spot, I'll simply let my mind relax as I travel about and stare out of a train or car window. Then I'll zone out. (Important note: not if I'm driving.)

Full disclosure: this wasn't an easy technique to pick up at first. After discovering dynamic meditation, I remember getting into the back of a taxi, where my first instinct was to check my phone for messages and social media updates, something we're all guilty of doing. But over time I trained myself to ignore any urges to scroll and text during quiet moments, and I relax my mind instead. It's a great way of calming myself down.

All you need to do is follow three simple steps:

1) **Put down the phone.**
2) **Clear your mind and stare out of a window.**
3) **Breathe slowly.**

With a little time, you'll feel much calmer.

Letting my brain relax in these moments has also helped me to land at some great ideas, or to find solutions for problems that have been winding me up. I've even used dynamic meditation at times of stress, when my teammates or colleagues have been arguing or if a project seemed to be on the verge of collapse. Rather than freaking out or rushing into an error I'd later regret, I meditated on the go, while plotting a logical way forward. In conflict, I'd learned how to remain calm in a gunfight, and thinking rationally saved my life on a few occasions. There's no reason why you can't do the same under less dangerous circumstances. Using this technique will help.

TACTICAL BRIEFING: TRUST THAT YOUR BEST IDEAS WILL STICK

There have been several occasions when I've run through a dynamic meditation and arrived at one or two great ideas (or, at least, I personally thought they were great). But rather than write them down, I've preferred to stay in the moment in the hope that something even better might come along. As a consequence, I've sometimes forgotten my initial 'moment of genius' and, having left the car and got to my front door, my mind has gone blank.

Fuck! I've thought. *Why didn't I write it down?*

At first this used to really bother me, but I've recently got into the habit of trusting that my best ideas will stick, without me needing to write them. Instead of getting down about a forgotten plan, I'll tell myself that any grand ideas I might have temporarily lost will return at some point in the near future. (The best ones always do.) When they don't, it's because my brain has edited them away for a reason.

⊙ THE LOOK FORWARD

You know what to do: on your next commute to work, or if you're in the back of an Uber after a night out, switch off your phone and take five minutes to do some dynamic meditation. And don't stress if a cracking idea comes to you in the moment and then disappears again. If it's any good, it will resurface later.

CHAPTER 4
SWITCHING ON

If you're a regular viewer of *SAS: Who Dares Wins*, there's every chance you'll have heard either one of my teammates or myself yelling a simple instruction at the recruits, over and over:

SWITCH ON!

When we shout this phrase – or a variation of it, such as *Get sparking!* or *Sharpen up!* – what we're asking of the individual is always unique to them. It really could be one of a million different things, but in essence we're trying to instil a positive sense of shock into someone who might have slowed down or fallen short. The hope is that they will react and dig themselves out of the hole they've stumbled into, or locate a better headspace in order to survive the course. A classic example would be the recruit who stumbles into a freezing-cold river or lake during an exercise. It's hammering down with rain; they're shivering and piss-wet through. And yet, for some reason, they're unable to motivate themselves to move away from trouble. Instead, they sit in the water and mope, not realizing that to remain static in such horrendous conditions only increases their chances of deteriorating physically.

Weirdly, I also notice this lethargic attitude in recruits when they're *not* doing any physical activities. Whenever the group returns to the dorm to briefly recover from whatever harshing we might have inflicted upon them, they all make the same mistake. Rather than keeping themselves busy, they'll crawl into a bunk and overthink their experience. They relive the pain of their last test and catastrophize the next challenge. And then they'll compare their performances against the efforts of the people around them. Inevitably, one or two of them will start feeling sorry for themselves. For those individuals, failure isn't too far away.

Whenever I've wandered into the sleeping quarters and noticed the group slumped in their bunks like zombies, I always deliver the same pep talk:

'The best thing you lot can do now is to stay busy in your head. Get a grip of yourself and keep your mind occupied. It will make you forget about all the bullshit that doesn't actually matter. Think about what we're going to be doing next – is your head set? Think about your kit – have you got everything packed? Think about hydration – are you drinking enough water? There's always something to do and there's always something to consider that's relevant to the next task. The minute you start focusing on a small, but important bit of admin, you'll switch on . . .'

We're all guilty of slipping into this shoddy state of mind from time to time, and it doesn't require a person to be in that much of an uncomfortable position for the brain to slow down. How many times have you sat on the edge of the bed on a cold morning and felt tired and mopey? You don't want to get ready, but rather than squaring away your personal admin you stare into space, unable to find the motivation required to move. It's at this point that you should be thinking about switching on.

BUT HOW?

This was a challenge I often had to overcome during my time in the military, because for long periods of time I was cold, wet and hungry, sometimes for days or weeks on end. Even getting into my sleeping bag was a minging experience sometimes: when camping in the rain, the material clung to my body. Some Commandos in those situations would get into a terrible state, and on every exercise I ever went on there was always one casualty – a bloke who looked to be on another planet emotionally and not yet synched with the environment or with the work ahead. Usually, one reminder from the lads nearby would be enough for them to find a more suitable level of alertness. Then they would get their heads in the game and press on with the work. If they couldn't, they were usually reprimanded, or binned off from the job. (But only if it had been a repeat offence.)

I quickly realized that in those situations I could choose only one of two strategies:

1) Grumble, fall apart and become a liability to both my teammates and myself.
2) Switch on and take my mental state to a position of alertness by imagining any future tasks ahead. This visualization was a distraction from the abject misery I was experiencing.

Really, I found that the best way of switching on was to remind myself of the consequences of *not* being fully present and alert in whatever I was doing. The process frightened me into raising my standards because I didn't want to fail. I also lifted my levels of situational awareness in the following ways:

- When I was stuck out in the cold and wet on an exercise or during Selection, I told myself that becoming comfortable with discomfort would set me apart from the other lads in my group.
- Whenever I operated at height or underwater and I felt too relaxed, I reminded myself that one miscalculated move might see me off in a pretty unpleasant way.
- If I sat at the end of my bunk after a morning shower,

> unable to move, I remembered that the inactivity
> would turn me into a useless bag of shit for the rest
> of the day and I'd fail to hit my targets.

These scares were always enough to get me sparking again.

TACTICAL BRIEFING: SWITCH ON, YOUR WAY

Switching on doesn't always require us to consider the worrying consequences of a lethargic or complacent attitude. In fact, there are all sorts of ways of getting the brain into gear for whatever task we're about to do. Take the following scenarios:

YOU NEED TO INCREASE YOUR FOCUS AT WORK

Start the day by reading a long news article very slowly and check in on yourself to see if you're paying attention. We live in a world where bite-sized chunks of information constantly compete for our attention, usually on our phones, where terms like 'TL; DR'* and 'BREAKING NEWS' have become the norm. According to neuroscientists from the Harvard University-affiliated Brigham and Women's Hospital, by reading a longer report slowly, and checking to see whether you've become distracted, you'll improve your monitoring processes when dealing with individual tasks.

YOU NEED TO BE SWITCHED ON AROUND OTHERS

Chat to a stranger when you're next queuing up for a coffee or waiting for the morning bus. Talking to someone you've never met

---

* TL; DR = Too long; don't read. You'll see this when the most important information from a long-form article has been distilled into a single tweet or thread.

before forces us to be fully present and engaged. It's also a good way to push us out of our comfort zone in a fairly benign environment. You might get a funny look or two, but that's their problem, not yours.

YOU NEED TO PREPARE FOR CHANGE

Maybe you've got a new job or you're about to move home. Inevitably there's going to be a period of upheaval where everything feels new and weird. Switch on in advance by changing up some of your regular routines. Rather than getting the same bus to work every day, cycle the route. Mix up your choice of supermarket on the grocery run. Train first thing in the morning rather than after work. Get the brain firing by doing everything you can to make the sense of unfamiliarity feel familiar.

⊕ THE LOOK FORWARD

When you feel yourself drifting, or you become distracted from the task in hand, consider the implications of remaining in a lethargic state. It might be that you're walking down an unfamiliar street at night with your headphones on, oblivious to the people around you. Imagine what might happen were someone to jump out at you from the shadows, or if you missed a shout for help. This should help to raise your situational awareness.

CHAPTER 5
STRESS AS AN ASSET

In times of chaos, it's an understandable human response to want to avoid negative emotions such as guilt, anger or fear. Sometimes we can even become fearful of experiencing fear itself. However, directly tackling these feelings can be a positive experience because it forces us to come out of hiding. This one move can reveal our true potential and encourage us to perform to the best of our ability. Trust me, I know: I've spent most of my life in a frightened state, firstly during the military and then throughout my second career on TV. I know from experience that I've grown as a person, having tackled a series of stressful situations head-on. I've also emerged from these events feeling considerably stronger and more confident.

A year or so ago, I did a bungee jump. Compared with some of the other challenges in my life, that might not seem like too much of a big deal, but believe me, it was. I'm on record as having an intense dislike of heights. They used to give me nightmares, though I've trained myself to harness the associated negative emotions. On this occasion I'd been asked to throw myself off the Newport Transporter Bridge in Wales for my show *Foxy's Fearless 48 Hours*. (Spoiler: the bridge is bloody high.) I was filming with the TV and radio presenter Maya Jama, and once the producers had sprung the challenge on me, I only had one response: *You wankers.* I'd never seen the point in doing a bungee jump before. *Why not do a parachute jump instead?* Now I was being asked to hurl myself off a 75-metre-high platform.

Well, it's not an ideal situation, I thought. *But I'll just have to turn my stress into an asset.*

Rather than focusing on how the upcoming test was a pain in the arse, I fell back on my military training. My job was to manage the emotions positively rather than allowing them to overwhelm me. While working at the sharp end of war, I'd learned that fear was a combat indicator, an early warning sign of some impending danger, and to overcome it I only had to recognize the stress for what it was: a hint that I should focus on the techniques required to perform to the best of my ability. I told myself that doing a bungee jump was fairly safe. It was certainly no more risky than dropping into an enemy compound during an operation, and I couldn't remember any of my teammates turning into a quivering wreck in those situations, so it wasn't going to happen to me on a bridge in Wales. By working through the task, step by step, and then moving as instructed, I felt confident I'd be fine.

I had to sit with this psychological challenge for two bloody days before the event. When the time to jump arrived, I successfully steadied myself – though it wasn't easy. For starters, I had to walk along a grated runway to the jumping point in the middle of the bridge. I felt like I was a mile up and it was possible to see the churning water of the River Usk below.

Bloody hell, I thought. *This is honking.*

I stepped towards the edge. The safety instructor clipped me into the bungee cord and delivered some final words of advice. Then I ramped up my aggression by sucking in several deep breaths. I focused on the pounding in my chest and used the sensation as fuel. *It was power.* From behind me, I heard a voice counting down:

Three . . .

My eyes glazed over, like a shark when it goes in for the kill.

Two . . .

I was in the zone.

One!

I flung myself forward, swallow-diving from the ledge as if I was jumping out of a plane. There was a split second of silence and then I heard the familiar roar of the wind as it buffeted my body, a sensation I'd experienced countless times in parachute training. By imagining I was engaged in a familiar activity, I found it easy to dissipate the fear. I even did a countdown in my head, as if I was waiting for a canopy to open.

One thousand . . .

Two thousand . . .

Three thousand . . .

The water rushed up at me. I felt the yank of the cord as my body was sucked up into the sky again. The horizon seemed to roll over on itself and my adrenaline buzzed. *Bungee jumping was awesome!* No joke: it was one of the best things I'd ever done, and if the crew had asked for a reshoot, I'd have happily gone through the experience again.

TACTICAL BRIEFING: RETHINK THE ENEMY

Anyone who claims they're not scared by moments of chaos or danger might well be a psychopath, or a liar. They're also overlooking one of the most powerful tools in the body's nervous system, because if we're able to harness fear rather than allowing it to overwhelm us, it's possible to become sharper and increasingly focused. In a TED Talk titled *How To Make Stress Your Friend*, Stanford University health psychologist Kelly McGonigal explains that when we're struck by fear, our heart rate rockets and the body's blood vessels tighten. Most people would consider this reaction to be worrying because these physiological conditions are known to be detrimental to our health in the long term. Certainly, chronic stress can lead to some pretty worrying heart conditions . . . *but only if we view the sensation as a negative.*

McGonigal explains how, during a Harvard University study, participants were asked to reframe how they viewed their physical responses to stress. Their cues were fairly simple:

- **If their breathing quickened, this was to be considered an asset:** *the brain was getting more oxygen.*
- **When their heart rate soared, this was a positive sign:** *their body was ready to perform.*

Not only did those people execute more effectively in a series of tasks, their blood vessels also remained relaxed.

'It actually looks a lot like what happens in moments of joy and courage,' said McGonigal of the response. 'Over a lifetime of stressful experiences, this one biological change could be the difference between a stress-induced heart attack at age fifty and living well into your nineties.'

While I was feeling edgy about my bungee jump, I'd viewed my physiological response as a net positive. My pounding heart was an engine ready to go; my rapid breathing was an indicator of peak performance; under stress, my senses had switched on and my concentration levels were at 100 per cent. As a result, I absorbed everything my instructor told me and, having followed his orders diligently, I was able to execute a task that had initially frightened me. I emerged from the test in better shape than I was before – I was a lot braver than I thought – and my confidence soared.

⊕ THE LOOK FORWARD

The next time you feel scared, worried or under pressure, reframe the stress by imagining your physiological reactions as an ally, rather than the enemy:

- Your heavy breathing before a blood test: *the brain is getting the oxygen it needs in order to thrive.*
- A pounding heart before an exam: *you're switched on and ready to perform.*
- The increase in body temperature that kicks in whenever bad news arrives: *your body's helping you to find a solution.*

Simply reimagining your physical state this way won't just help you to function under pressure, it might just help you to live longer too.

CHAPTER 6
COMMAND YOUR DIGITAL BATTLESPACE

The definition of what actually constitutes a battlefield has changed massively over the last hundred years or so. Once regarded as a literal field of mud, trenches and reels of barbed wire, the theatre of conflict has since been transformed into a *battlespace* – a four-dimensional war zone comprising land, sea, air and even the cyber landscape. It's within these regions that hostilities will kick off, or a nation state might attempt to gain a series of strategic and tactical advantages over their enemy. With cyber warfare now an increasingly common form of aggression, it's also possible for our digital resources, such as smartphones, social media accounts and email addresses, to be turned against us.

This was already becoming an issue during my time in the military elite. I remember ten years ago, while readying ourselves for a domestic drug bust on the Thames, our commanding officer had locked away the lads' personal devices in a secure box. It was suspected that the people we were closing in on possessed the technology to detect our mobiles. Elsewhere, during the War on Terror, we always established radio silence while approaching a target or a compound. Having reached a certain proximity to the enemy, the group's non-essential communications were shut down so that our arrival would remain undetected by any patrolling gunmen. This tactic also prevented anyone from listening in and overhearing a snippet of valuable intelligence, something that might tip the odds against us during the impending scrap.

Our processes were always clear: during missions, our comms and technology were regarded as vital assets, but if we were careless, that same technology had the potential to bring us down. This attitude has since proved invaluable out of war, but for very different reasons. Like most people, I'm connected to my personal comms for large chunks of the day; I'll scroll through Facebook, post Twitter updates for work and connect with mates on WhatsApp. For the most part I'll remain unaffected by what I'm reading, especially if it's critical, but if my head's on fire with stress I sometimes notice a negative reaction from overusing various online apps. I'm not alone. For those of us that are in a bad place emotionally, it's very easy to become upended by phone-related FOMO, anger and/or anxiety, not to mention a creeping sense of helplessness.

And it feels shit.

Before I go any further, I'd like to point out that I'm not against smartphones – they're an invaluable resource for all sorts of reasons. It's just that many digital services, tools and apps have been developed to 'hook' their subscribers in to using them again and again. (Have you noticed that the spinning disc on some messaging services even resembles a roulette wheel? The similarities in design are deliberate.) Elsewhere, news sites seem primed to rile everybody up, and social media platforms have hijacked our attention spans. This environment is fairly benign for an individual in a good headspace, but during times of chaos, all that compulsive swiping and scrolling can become a debilitating business. Our brains would be better served resting, or figuring out the very problem that's turned our world upside down in the first place.

The reality is that all those online hits, clicks and likes can create a chemical imbalance in the head. Neuroscientists have discovered that the brain's pain and pleasure receptors are located alongside one another. Importantly, they work like a set of old-school measuring scales, with pleasure on one side, and pain the other. According to Dr Anna Lembke, the author of *Dopamine Nation: Finding Balance in the Age of Indulgence*, this system craves neutrality. In other words: if we go online and see that our latest picture has gathered a record number of likes and comments, the scales will tip in the direction of 'pleasure'. Once logged off, those same scales will droop towards the side of 'pain' in an equal amount. A balance is eventually restored, but the process is uncomfortable.

'It's like a falling-away,' explained Dr Lembke in an interview on *The Huberman Lab* podcast in 2021. 'You're on social media. You get a good tweet and then you can't stop yourself because there's this awareness, this latent awareness, that as soon as you stop engaging with the behaviour, you're going to experience a pain, a falling-away, a missing of that feeling, and a wanting more of it.'

But there is a way to redress the balance.

TACTICAL BRIEFING: TRAFFIC-LIGHT YOUR VULNERABILITY

One technique that works when managing a high level of digital stress is to command the battlespace on your phone through a series of tactical assessments. To do so, first establish your state of mind – good, OK or bad – and then adjust how you engage with the tech accordingly. Think of this process as a traffic-light system:

GREEN: YOU'RE FEELING STRONG

Go, but proceed carefully. Square away your digital admin. Use any periods of calm to track the amount of time spent on your devices. Most phones will record the owner's daily online activity, so a quick check-in should reveal which apps you're using the most and for how long. *You're spending an hour a day with a workout app?* Awesome. But if you're shocked to discover that several whole days in a year have been dedicated to TikTok, it might be time for a rethink.

AMBER: YOU'RE FEELING WOBBLY

Pause for a moment. Set up your defences and assess which of your apps are helpful and which are harmful. For example, an armoury of self-help, fitness and psych apps should be considered a major asset, but any online distractions, such as games, gambling sites and social media could be regarded as being potentially hostile because they have the ability to put a person into a tailspin. The same can be said of news apps; it's better to avoid the bombardment of depressing headlines when your world is turning to shit. Swipe through the phone and decide whether each of your apps is a friend or enemy.

Once everything has been categorized, put your most used apps into one of two folders – ASSET or HOSTILE. Send the HOSTILE folder deep into your phone – two or three swipes away from the home screen should do the trick. These distractions can then remain out of sight until you've returned to a GREEN state of mind. Similarly, give priority to the ASSET apps. These resources should remain on your home screen so they're within easy reach at all times.

RED: FRAZZLED

Pump the brakes. The most widely prescribed solution to a phone-related meltdown is the digital detox, a brutal act of self-discipline in which our most destructive apps are deleted and our devices are hidden away for hours on end. There are even retreats where people can detach from their phones for lengthier periods of time. I've also heard of people reverting to their old 2010 Nokia or Samsung 'dumbphones' in order to disconnect from the internet – their digital-related issues having become so unbearable.

When we're in a RED state, it's important to boost the protective steps mentioned in the GREEN and AMBER phases with a series of positive manoeuvres. This could include leaving your phone outside the bedroom at night and not using it until after breakfast, or creating tech-free spaces and events throughout the day. (Ban the phone from your dinner table; put the phone in another room when you're watching a film.) Setting an alarm that reminds you to grab thirty minutes of fresh air, away from your phone, is a healthy adjustment; by tweaking your phone's settings (on some models), it's possible to establish blockers, or time limits on certain apps, so that you'll be locked out of them if your usage becomes excessive. It can also help to have a photo of a supportive loved one as your screen saver.

For too long, technology has tried to hijack our attention spans, sometimes to the detriment of our mental well-being. But by commanding our digital battlespace, it's possible to regain tactical control and find balance in times of emotional upheaval.

⊖ THE LOOK FORWARD

Turn your phone screen to black and white to make it a less seductive distraction. To do this on an iPhone follow these steps:

1) **Head to SETTINGS.**
2) **Select ACCESSIBILITY.**
3) **Select DISPLAY AND TEXT SIZE.**
4) **Select COLOUR FILTERS.**
5) **Enable COLOUR FILTERS.**
6) **Choose GREYSCALE.**

Your phone will now take on a variety of dull, and less addictive, shades of grey. Don't worry: you can toggle back to your original set-up quite easily once you feel less frazzled. (I have to credit the comedians and actors Romesh Ranganathan and Tom Davis, who first mentioned this trick on their Wolf & Owl podcast.) This doesn't just work on iPhones either and a number of other phone manufacturers have added this setting should you wish to use it.

CHAPTER 7
THE TINY DETAILS

Nimsdai Purja, my colleague from the military elite and a man famous for climbing the fourteen 'death zone' mountains in the record-breaking time of six months, once claimed that it's the little things that count the most on the big mountains. In other words: the issues that may seem insignificant at base camp (a leaky water bottle, a poorly fixed boot) will probably bite you on the arse when you're higher up, where the air is perilously thin and the smallest efforts can be exhausting. For example, a mountaineer with a loose boot will have to remove their glove to adjust it and this might take them several minutes. Without gloves, their hands will become frostbitten and the already dangerous process of climbing up or down will become impossible. Suddenly the mountaineer is stranded, and a problem that was easily resolved at sea level has become a death sentence.

A similar approach prevailed during my time in the British Armed Forces. There, my personal focus was performing the basics to an elite standard, even when under serious pressure. I first adopted this mindset in the Royal Marines and then carried it into Selection for the military elite, where my attitude set me apart from some of my peers. I learned very quickly that being a specialist asset wasn't all about abseiling out of helicopters and kicking down doors – although that definitely played a part – but had everything to do with being meticulous and safe when performing the everyday tasks, such as shooting, movement, and camouflage and concealment, as follows.

SHOOTING

So many people failed Selection because they were too lazy, or too frazzled, to use their weapon's sight when firing it. Others failed to put their safety catch on between exercises, or they neglected to clean their weapon properly while resting in camp. These were major red flags for the watching DS. As far as they were concerned, a recruit who neglected to use his sight was going through the motions and therefore sloppy. The individual who failed to use his safety catch was a risk to himself and the people around him. And the bloke who didn't take care of his weapon was likely to see it jam at the worst possible moment. These details, while tiny, were potentially fatal in combat and overlooking them was enough to see a candidate binned off.

MOVEMENT

In certain environments, it was vital that an operator took extra care when moving covertly. For example, whenever I was navigating jungle terrain, I had to pay special attention to where I was stepping and what obstacles might lie ahead. An individual who crashed through the foliage without giving a toss, breaking branches and leaving easily tracked footprints, would only alert a tracker to their presence and their route; heavy boots tended to snap brittle tree limbs with a loud crack, which was another giveaway. During Selection, I can remember one member of the DS shouting at my patrol that he didn't want any *jungle buffoonery*. What he meant was that we needed to pay attention to the tiny details if we were to pass the course.

CAMOUFLAGE AND CONCEALMENT

An elite soldier will quickly come a cropper if they fail to mask their position while on an operation, and whenever I was on a patrol where it was vital I remained unseen, I'd make sure to wear a base layer that took away my natural skin colour's 'shine'. I also covered up the lines in my face before camouflaging the rest of my kit, so no straight lines were visible (because there are no straight lines in woodland or on a mountain.) I even took extra care when camouflaging my position while on watch. When operating in a jungle environment, it was no good grabbing a load of foliage from one place and then dragging it to another. If the foliage didn't match the immediate surroundings, my hidey-hole would become compromised very quickly because it would look bloody weird.

TACTICAL BRIEFING: KIT HUSBANDRY

Individuals who don't look after the tiny details in their life will nearly always fall into serious trouble at some point. Sure, during periods of calm they'll usually get away with a certain amount of corner-cutting. However, when things turn hectic, those tiny details will likely trip them up in all sorts of ways, often when they least expect it. You probably know at least one person who habitually fails to check their travel details in advance of an important work trip, or leaves their holiday packing/Christmas shopping/tax return to the very last minute. Taken individually, these examples aren't that big a deal. But these minor issues will soon get in the way of the bigger life stuff if procrastination or slack thinking is a common theme in that person's life.

From the minute I started with the Royal Marines, I was taught the importance of looking after the smallest details so that I could concentrate on the important job of being a commando. I was even informed that by turning up on time I was actually arriving late – I instead had to be in the relevant area, settled and ready, ahead of time if I was to be considered prepared. I also kept a diligent eye on my kit and weapon at all times, and made sure that I was properly hydrated and well fed. Considering these small points meant I had more time in which to become a resilient force, with zero distractions.

All of us can apply this attitude to our daily routines, though. It doesn't take a genius to work out where we can be sharper and more efficient; we just have to find the motivation to do it. Techniques that can help us in this area include:

- List-making: Write down what you need to achieve the next day and get to it.
- Get up earlier: If you need more time, make it for yourself.
- Quit multitasking: Focus on one thing only.
- Embrace the grind: Prioritize the job you hate the most so it's out of the way early.

⊛ THE LOOK FORWARD

Analyse your daily routines and separate them into categories, such as work, nutrition, home and exercise. Then work out one small detail you can attend to in order to improve the mechanics of each category. Next, pay attention to how your performance levels change. For example:

- Work: Tidy your desk at the end of every shift so it's set up for the next day.
- Nutrition: Meal-plan and batch-cook every Sunday.
- Home: While cleaning your teeth, do a small domestic task, or perform a set of squats.

- **Exercise: Ready your kit the night before your next gym session.**

Making these small but effective changes will have a major impact on the structure of your day because a) your tasks will be executed more effectively and with less stress, and b) these small tweaks will become habitual and encourage you to improve your performance in other areas.

CHAPTER 8
NEGATIVES TO POSITIVES

At the elite level of any organization, whether that's in business, sport, finance or the military, there's no such thing as a negative event. Instead, any moments of failure, loss, shock or pain are treated as learning experiences whereby the individuals involved can grow and become stronger. If that sounds crazy, let me recall some of the shit situations I've found myself in, and the way in which I've reframed them.

NEGATIVE EXPERIENCE	POSITIVE RESPONSE
I'm getting divorced.	I have a chance to start again and meet someone more suited to my personality.
A friend has been killed.	I can spend time reflecting on the positive impact that person has had on me. The loss will help me to appreciate the friendships I still have.
I've lost a job I loved.	I can spend time finding a new purpose.
I'm injured.	I can spend some time learning new skills. Once I'm healed I can work on making myself even stronger.

NEGATIVES TO POSITIVES

This technique can be applied to just about any situation, even fear of death. (Positive response: I won't be around to experience it, so why should I be worried?) I think I was able to approach adversity this way because to act with negative thought in military service was a debilitating psychological position. My role was to work in terrifying situations where I was expected to operate effectively at all times. If I suddenly decided to mope around because my team was getting shot at or because we'd been ordered to traipse 50km to a position in horrendous conditions, I'd likely become a liability within the group and possibly fail in some way that might see me off permanently.

I've made this reframing tactic a major part of my latest career, where I often work with people who don't think like a military operator. One such instance took place a while back, when I was working in a very dangerous location abroad and it had become clear at least one member of the production crew was feeling emotionally out of their depth. Given that they'd understood the risks prior to taking part, this should have been an opportunity for them to grow, but instead they became bogged down by negatives. Then they spun out. There were miscommunications with our series producer back in London, and the resulting crossed wires then led one or two people to bicker in the field. (That in itself could have been considered a danger, given where we were working.) Rather than panicking, I pulled the team together, hoping to become the conduit between the groups on the ground and in London. I then viewed the chaos as an educational opportunity:

- **Communication was everything:** I was learning that all channels needed to be open, and at all times, when following a filming schedule in a sketchy environment.
- **I had to get involved across all aspects of the production:** Some TV presenters are wheeled out to

> speak to the cameras, after which they go home. The
> type of shows I worked on didn't allow for that style of
> delivery. They required total engagement in all areas,
> from the team's safety protocols to the presentation,
> and I needed to be on the ball at all times.

Rather than sulking, or moaning about how everything was falling apart, I got stuck in and turned a precarious situation into a positive one. Then I did everything I could to bring calm to a chaotic shoot. In the process, I became more experienced in what, and what not, to do in a new line of work.

TACTICAL BRIEFING: USE YOUR FAILURES AS ROCKET FUEL

Consider these famous examples of failure:

- Best-selling author Stephen King was rejected by thirty publishers after writing his first novel, *Carrie*.
- Oscar-winning director Steven Spielberg was rejected from the University of Southern California's film school three times.
- Basketball star Michael Jordan failed to make his high school's varsity team.

Do you think these individuals moped around for weeks on end in the aftermath of failure? Or spent their days wasting countless mental calories with negative self-talk? *Did they bollocks*. Stephen King eventually sold *Carrie* and became one of the world's most famous writers and Spielberg produced some of the greatest films of all time. Meanwhile, Jordan became a living legend. In a famous advert for Nike called *Failure*, he even highlighted his screw-ups:

'I've missed more than 9,000 shots in my career. I've lost almost 300 games. Twenty-six times, I've been trusted to take the game- winning shot – and missed. I've failed over and over and over again in my life. And that is why I succeed.'

There was someone who knew how to turn a negative situation into a positive experience. Jordan was kicked in the swingers over and over, only to stand up and have another pop.

And you should do the same.

Why? Because by connecting positive thought to negative events we can create get-out-of-jail-free cards for ourselves; the process frees us from the shackles of a setback. There is even scientific evidence to suggest that reframing a grim situation as something positive can help an individual to grow in all sorts of ways. In a 2004 paper entitled *The Broaden-and-Build Theory of Positive Emotions*, positive-psychology researcher Barbara L. Fredrickson explained how thinking with positivity can lead to the following:

- **Expanding thought–action repertoires – in other words, people become more creative, flexible and efficient.**
- **Negative emotions are counteracted.**
- **Mental resilience is increased.**
- **A person's overall mental and physical well-being is improved.**

All of which makes a good case for reimagining a crap sandwich as a Michelin-starred feast.

⊕ THE LOOK FORWARD

Below, recall some of the negatives that have taken place in your life and regard them as a learning experience, even if they may have been horrendously painful at the time. Then work on transforming this style of thinking into a habitual practice. For example, someone grabs the last sandwich in a café – *your favourite sandwich*. The positive? You can go for the much healthier salad instead. If you can become comfortable in thinking this way, you'll become happier, sharper and much stronger as a result.

NEGATIVE EXPERIENCE	POSITIVE RESPONSE
EXAMPLE 1	
EXAMPLE 2	
EXAMPLE 3	

CHAPTER 9
SLOW IS SMOOTH, SMOOTH IS FAST

The phrase 'Slow is smooth, smooth is fast' is constantly bandied about in the military, especially during weapon-training drills and exercises. The reason for using this mantra is clear: when a group of individuals is learning a new skill, they tend to want to get to the ending very quickly – the moment where they're operating with maximum efficiency. This is a mistake we're all guilty of making from time to time, whether we're learning how to fire a weapon, throw a punch in the boxing ring or form a clay vase at the pottery wheel. The problem, as the military have long understood, is that rushing to the end of a task isn't actually a speedy way of doing things. People cut corners, mistakes are made and everything turns to shit very quickly. Instead, their solution is to encourage the individuals learning in their care to go slowly, because it tends to bring better results, ahead of time.

I've recently taken up golf, which is probably one of the most frustrating sports for a beginner because everything feels so complex and nerve-racking. Teeing off on the first hole does my head in, especially if I'm doing it in front of a line of other people waiting to play. It's horrible. I've noticed that I have a tendency to feel that I'm being judged, and when I first started the game my natural instinct was to rush my first tee shot in an attempt to get it over and done with. I raced through the process, grabbing my club without thinking. Then I'd hit the skin off the ball as hard as I could without considering my target or taking a practice swing. Inevitably,

I'd screw the shot into the trees – that's if I managed to connect with it at all – and the search for my ball would then hold up the growing queue of now-frustrated golfers standing behind me.

I soon learned that in order to speed things up, I actually had to do everything a lot more slowly. By standing over the ball and visualizing where I wanted it to go, I was able to set myself correctly. By taking a practice swing, I could loosen up and lean into muscle memory. And by thinking about tempo rather than brute force, I found it easier to connect with the ball. While I'm still not hitting the fairway every time, by slowing down I can at least hold my own, and these days I spend less time in the rough – or worse, in the woods – which speeds up my progress around the course.

It's easy to succumb to this mindset in times of chaos. We find ourselves in a tricky spot – either one of our own making or due to something beyond our control – and we want to get to the ending – the bit where everything is sorted and we've returned to a state of equilibrium. But the problem with rushing in stressful situations is that we then become erratic, and make even more trouble for ourselves.

A classic example of this situation is the frazzled car journey. A person is late for a commitment – maybe it's their fault, maybe it's not – and in a desperate attempt to make up the time, they put their foot on the accelerator and race to the final destination while taking a series of risks. I see raging motorists in London all the time; they're so eager to get somewhere that they act like a dick and cut people up in traffic. The problem with that type of situation is that it rarely gets a person anywhere. I can't remember the number of times someone has torn away from me at the traffic lights in an attempt to shave a few seconds off their journey, only for me to pull up alongside them at the next junction. The only difference between them and me is that they've operated recklessly and taken a chance with their safety and that of the other drivers around them. (And an accident is only going to slow them down and ruin their day.) Meanwhile, I've gone along at my own speed, knowing that slow is smooth, smooth is fast.

TACTICAL BRIEFING: SMILE IN SUFFERING

A good way of improving our performance in times of chaos or stress is to stop for a second and . . . *smile*. I used this technique in all sorts of terrifying situations when the bullets were flying around or things were blowing up nearby. There were times in combat when a round whistled by my head, but rather than yelling in terror or shouting out for help, I dived for cover with my teammates and then laughed about it. Really, there was no point in getting angry or scared. That wasn't going to help in a situation where somebody was trying to kill me.

It's widely believed that smiling not only helps to alleviate stress in times of chaos, but can also speed up our recovery after an unpleasant event. When we grin or laugh, hits of endorphins and serotonin are released, which lift our mood and improve our emotional state. Meanwhile, the physical act of laughter actually creates a calming effect because it relaxes our muscles, has a positive effect on the body's circulation, and improves our heart rate and blood pressure. If that isn't enough to convince you, consider this stat: according to researchers from the Hewlett-Packard Development Company, one grin can deliver the same level of activity in the brain's reward centre as 2,000 chocolate bars. So slow down for a second and have a laugh. It could be your greatest ally.

→ THE LOOK FORWARD

In a moment of discomfort, or when you're trying to work slowly and smoothly, take a moment to find some humour in the situation:

- When you're cranking through the push-ups in a gruelling workout, laugh at the pain.
- When learning a new skill, take a step back and smile at the fact that you're testing yourself.
- When working under pressure, or through fear, find some humour in the situation, no matter how grim it may seem at the time.

CHAPTER 10
AVOIDING BURNOUT

Author's note: While this book is designed to be read either from cover to cover, in scenario-relevant chunks or at random, it's important that the next four chapters are considered as a whole. When dealing with serious mental health issues, it's hard to spot the warning signs. For that reason, some of the advice I'm about to give you will feel fairly straightforward. But that's because it's hard to put one foot in front of the other when it seems as if your life is falling apart.

Regardless of your present emotional condition, please take some time to absorb the advice that I've gathered here. Yes, you may feel emotionally strong at the moment, but it only takes one event to push a person towards burnout or rock bottom, and the first jolt can come out of nowhere. Even if you're going along just fine yourself, the following lessons will help you to spot trouble in a friend or family member. Learning how to recognize the symptoms and encouraging a person to get help can be a game-changer in some cases.

In a post-Covid world, where the cost-of-living crisis has hit everyone hard, the concept of burnout has become familiar when describing a person's state of mind. In moments of chaos it's not uncommon for an individual to feel emotionally beasted – over-worked, underpaid and pushed to the limit with stress. According to the NHS, burnout is 'a state of physical and emotional exhaustion.

It can occur when you experience long-term stress in your job, or when you have worked in a physically or emotionally draining role for a long time.' In 2021, a survey conducted by The King's Fund concluded that their employees were approximately 50 per cent more likely to suffer from 'chronic stress', which is known to be a precursor to becoming burned out.* This has serious blowback on patient care, staff well-being and institutional finances, because when an employee is feeling burned out, they usually call in sick or underperform on the job.

Working for the military was an equally stressful vocation, even though the top dogs did everything they could to prevent us from breaking down. This was a tricky balancing act for the lads involved, because we were, on occasions, removed from the thick of the action and put into different roles that meant we could keep our minds and bodies sharp. I hated this phase in the cycle. We all did. Being out of the theatre of combat meant FOMO, and that tended to wind me up.

I remember one year when I was serving at home when the work looked like it should have been fun: I was training lads who were on Selection and hanging out with my friends. But behind the scenes my life was a mess. I was in the thick of a messy break-up with my wife and I then found myself in another complicated relationship. Meanwhile, my head was all over the place. All I could think about was getting back on tour with the lads and being in the thick of the action again. In the end, two positions opened up in a pioneering capability and the group needed volunteers to fill the roles. I stuck my hand up and got the gig, even though I didn't really want to do it – I just wanted to be back in the game. With hindsight, this was a massive mistake. I wasn't in the right place emotionally for the work, but I believed that going back into war would act as a distraction from the personal issues that were weighing me down. Inevitably

* This figure is thought to be as high as 85 per cent in the financial sector.

it all became too much. Before long, I began displaying the classic symptoms of burnout, but I didn't pay any attention to them.

Shortly afterwards, I fell apart.

TACTICAL BRIEFING: HOW TO SPOT BURNOUT (AND WHAT TO DO)

Burnout is a relentless enemy. According to researchers, its more serious symptoms include heart conditions, depression and hypertension. Often people facing burnout will numb their pain with booze or drugs, and if left untreated these negative conditions can have a serious effect on a person's home and work lives. In their book *The Burnout Challenge: Managing People's Relationships With Their Jobs*, the authors, social psychologist Christina Maslach and organizational psychologist Michael P. Leiter, explain there are three components of burnout: exhaustion, cynicism and inefficacy.

- **Exhaustion:** You feel knackered. It's hard to focus on the job in hand even when it's a task you ordinarily love.
- **Cynicism:** You emotionally disconnect from the thing that's burning you out. This happens because the brain is putting up its armour. You behave negatively towards whatever it is you're working on and the people you're working with.
- **Inefficacy:** You fall into an emotional tailspin. Every choice and action is questioned. You second-guess your abilities and doubt your chances of finishing a task on time.

While these symptoms can feel debilitating in the moment, they are treatable, as I'll explain. My problem during my final, frantic year of service was that I ignored the warning lights of burnout. I was knackered and as a result I later fell out of love with the job and stopped looking after myself. Then I became racked with self-doubt. But still I pushed ahead. When PTSD later kicked in, I was unable to cope and unravelled completely. Maybe if I had paid attention to the early signals of burnout and taken action, I might not have fallen so hard – it's hard to tell. What I have learned is that it's possible to manage the impact of burnout with the implementation of a few techniques.

1) RE-EVALUATE YOUR PRIORITIES

If a personal project is impacting your health, step away for a while. If work is causing you to spin out, take some time off or establish a few healthy boundaries to protect your recovery time. (One option might be to not check work-related emails outside of office hours.) If you're feeling overwhelmed by a combination of social, family and other commitments, prioritize the ones that are most important to you and become comfortable with saying 'no'.

2) CHECK IN WITH YOUR BROTHER-/SISTERHOOD

If you're feeling close to burnout, make regular contact with your mates and close family members (unless they're the cause of your stress). Not only will they provide support, but you'll clarify your situation by spending time with the important people in your life.

3) TAKE TIME TO RECOVER

Make sure to do whatever you can to distance yourself from the people or circumstances that have caused you to crash. Appreciate your experience. Perform a self-analysis. (See Part

Two, Chapter 2.) Spend time in nature. Do the things that make you happy. You might argue that your workload or personal circumstances won't allow for it. I'd argue that the more serious symptoms of burnout are too dangerous to ignore.

⊕ THE LOOK FORWARD

Take control of your stressors. To do so, first list the things that are causing you the biggest headaches. Then establish a plan to resolve each one. Some might be easy to resolve; others may require a more concerted effort – for example, a dispute with a colleague or business partner that has created significant friction in the workplace. At the very least, drawing up a list will give you a sense of control in a scary situation. From there you can take small steps towards recovery. My advice: like credit-card debt, it's best to tackle the smaller, more easily fixable balances first. Any lightening of the load will only improve matters.

CHAPTER 11
RECOGNIZING
ROCK BOTTOM

With hindsight, my rock-bottom moment was fairly obvious. It was 2013. I was standing at a cliff edge in the pissing rain, staring down at the rocks and raging sea below, wondering whether I should throw myself off. The events that had led me there had sparked warning signs, but I'd paid zero attention to them. Having been diagnosed with PTSD, I was medically discharged from the military and ended up working in a civilian job that required me to drive around the south coast a lot. I often found myself pulling over in a motorway lay-by to have a meltdown or to cry my eyes out. Elsewhere, my latest relationship was a nightmare and I didn't want to go home. I was fed up with life and wanted it to change – or to end. Thank God I pushed for change.

Rock bottom is hard to spot when you're the person landing there. I remember having a rough go of it in the year or so prior to experiencing those suicidal thoughts. I hadn't wanted to leave the military, partly because I'd loved the job, but also because the intensity of my work was providing a distraction from the war zone that was my personal life. And though I experienced moments of intense fear, detachment and depression while scrapping abroad, I didn't want it to end for good; I wanted my brain to be patched up so I could get back to work again. (Little did I know at the time how much of a long old process that would be.) To compound matters, all of this was taking place in the year after my first marriage had fallen apart, and though my then wife and I still got on (and had made a go of repairing the damage between us), we both knew it was over. She would later end up seeing one of the lads in my unit and there was no hiding place from my pain.

I was thirty-five at the time and I remember being really down on myself. Then the negative self-talk turned nuclear.

I'm never going to meet anyone again. I'm shit. No one's going to want me.

Once I'd left the military, my inner critic decided to kick me in the balls – over and over.

You couldn't keep hold of the one thing you were good at. You're weak. It's finished.

I briefly landed a job in a bar, pulling pints and wiping down tables. I *hated* it. I wanted to be anywhere else and it showed. One afternoon, I remember standing in the middle of the place, staring into the distance and not thinking about anything. I wasn't having an episode, like the kind you see on TV, where a sufferer with some mental health issue relives the trigger points of their trauma. Instead, I had zoned out, which is a classic symptom of PTSD. One of the girls I worked with tugged at my arm.

'Foxy, are you alright?' she said.

'Yeah. Why?'

'You looked a million miles away, like you weren't even on this planet.'

'I'm fine.'

But I wasn't, and the alarm bells that I might be approaching rock bottom were intensifying:

Clang! I lived in a beautiful coastal town, but it might as well have been a battlespace in the middle of nowhere. I was desperately unhappy.

Clang! I loved travelling about but I never wanted to get to where I was going.

Clang! I'd call people in the middle of the night and cry down the phone. The next day I wouldn't remember the conversation.

One day, while driving home from my new office job, I decided that enough was enough. *Fuck my life*, I thought, and headed towards the coast, pulling over in a car park overlooking the cliffs. It was pissing down with rain and blowing a gale. I was wearing a suit and a shitty pair of trainers as I trudged towards the edge and peered down. *Would anyone care if I jumped?* I didn't know; I was that depressed. But when I thought long and hard about my life, I knew it couldn't end there – I had too much to scrap for. By staring suicide in the face, I finally recognized that I was at rock bottom. I then told myself that there had to be a way out of the hole I'd fallen into. I only had to figure out what that way actually was.

Fuck this, I thought. *I'm turning around.*

I couldn't wait to get back in the car.

TACTICAL BRIEFING: THE RECONNAISSANCE FROM ROCK BOTTOM

When discussing rock bottom, therapists will list a series of indicators we should all be paying attention to, either in ourselves or in others. The most commonly mentioned are:

- Suicidal thoughts and feelings of hopelessness.
- Detachment from friends and family.
- A decline in performance levels at work.
- Numbing an unseen pain through booze, drugs. or other stimulants.
- Over- or under-sleeping.
- Extreme mood swings.

But every person is different, and rock bottom can manifest itself in all sorts of ways. One individual might become unexpectedly violent after a few drinks; another will lose themselves in a gambling binge. Others will suffer alone and in silence. But in all cases, the key to moving away from the lowest point is to recognize where the problem has actually stemmed from in the first place, though that's easier said than done. Thankfully, therapy can help with this fact-finding mission.

In my experience, the source point for most emotional traumas can usually be found in at least one of the following three areas: love, money or work. A person need only experience trauma in one of these categories to fall hard, though, as I know, it's not uncommon for someone to suffer on multiple levels.

LOVE

I had pinged from one toxic relationship to another in the wake of my collapsed marriage. As a result, my head was in a mess, which only amplified my PTSD. For other people, depression and extreme anxiety can be caused by a multitude of scenarios linked to love and these can include the death of a close friend or family member, an abusive spouse, a painful breach of trust, or pre-mourning (the pain that occurs when a person close to you is dying slowly). These situations are incredibly distressing and it's not uncommon for someone in the midst of one of them to feel broken and very alone.

MONEY

I was OK on the cash front once I'd retired from the military. Of course I could have done with a few more quid, but I was lucky; not everyone is financially stable, and we're living in an age of financial chaos, with huge shifts in inflation, house prices and energy bills. Meanwhile, homelessness is on the up and people are losing their jobs left, right and centre. If managed poorly, financial stress can feel like a boot on the throat and it's a major cause of mental health issues that we should all be on the look-out for.

WORK
....

A major part of my life went up in smoke once I'd left the British Armed Forces. I moved away from mates, the routines I had relied upon for stability fell apart and I lost my sense of purpose. With nothing to get up for in the morning, my motivation drained away and I turned into a bag of shit. I stopped looking after myself and started drinking heavily. In the end I took a job that I was completely unsuited to and it made me miserable. Along with everything else that was going on, this situation was another layer of pain.

Most of us will spend large chunks of our life at work, so it's important we find a role that brings us satisfaction on some level. If we don't, we'll likely become miserable. On the other hand, when we lose that foundation in our life through redundancy, injury or illness, it can feel like a loss of identity and this can then bring feelings of grief, anger or shame. Even when we're working in a position we love, work-related conditions such as stress, a lack of sleep, or burnout, can drag us down, too.

If you're struggling in any of these areas, or you know someone who is, keep an eye out for the warning signs. Rock bottom is a scary place to be and nobody can get out of it alone.

⊕ THE LOOK FORWARD

If you feel you're at rock bottom, or approaching it, ask for help. *No excuses.* It will probably save your life. Likewise, if you see a person close to you approaching their lowest point, encourage them to seek professional advice.

CHAPTER 12
ASKING FOR HELP

I'll keep this lesson short and sweet. When it comes to asking for help, there's really no standard operating procedure for how to begin. *You just have to rip off the Band-Aid and do it.* Believe me, I know from experience how terrifying this one act can be. At my lowest point, it required me to admit to having an emotional weakness, something I'd been almost conditioned not to accept in the military. But I knew that there was no way of simply gritting my teeth and pushing through the pain this time – I had to raise my hand. Then I asked for help. As a result, my ego took a kicking, but thank God it did. By getting the assistance I so badly needed, I was able to rebuild my life.

Through that experience, I've learned several simple facts about asking for help:

- You *will* have to take a deep dive into your reality, which is a scary thing to do.
- You *will* have to accept that you're in a bad way.
- You *will* have to be vulnerable and front up to someone.
- You *will* feel shit about it at first.
- You *will* feel the weight coming off once you've done it.

So, fuck your pride. Fuck your reputation. Fuck the feelings of others. If you've hit rock bottom, or you're close to burning out, get the help you so badly need.

TACTICAL BRIEFING: TIDY THE FIRST CORNER

The one piece of advice I would give to my younger self – the broken man in a shit state – would be to chat to just one person at first, rather than taking in a string of different opinions, because you'll only hear a million ideas on how to fix the problem:

'You need to change this.'
'You need to stop doing that.'
'You need to go here. You need to go there.'

You'll be bombarded with so much information that it will most likely do your head in. You might become overwhelmed, which will only tempt you to give up on straightening yourself out before you've even started. Instead, I've found it helps to consider the problem as you would a messy house. Rather than tackling the whole place all at once – because that can be just as overwhelming – it's better to pick one corner and begin the tidying there, working square metre by square metre until some progress becomes apparent. This same approach works when tidying the head. Don't worry about the problem as a whole, focus on one small thing to get you started. For example, find someone who can help, whether it's a friend, a family member or a professional. And then talk.

⊙ THE LOOK FORWARD

When it comes to asking for assistance, don't worry about detailing the starting point of how you got to be where you are. Simply explain the position you're currently in. Every corner in the house will get tidied in its own time. You just need to start the healing process by opening up.

CHAPTER 13

THE TRUTH ABOUT THERAPY

There's zero doubt in my mind that therapy has saved my life. With the help of two counsellors, I was able to extract myself from a situation in which I could see no way forward. I was lost, moving without purpose and heading towards a nasty ending. But after a period of professional help, my thinking was rewired and I picked up an armoury of tools that would later help me to better navigate any future moments of stress and depression. At the same time, I've realized that it's OK to feel sad, worried and angry in times of chaos. Just because I was feeling shit, it didn't make me a weak person. If anything, learning from those emotions, while understanding how to manage them in times of chaos, allowed me to grow and has given me an extra layer of armour.

If you're considering going to therapy, for whatever reason, I definitely recommend you give it a try, especially if the symptoms of rock bottom are making themselves apparent. If you're in a bad place, there's really no better way to un-fuck yourself than by chatting to an expert about it, though I can guarantee that it will be a weird experience at first. You'll feel awkward, vulnerable and maybe even a little bit embarrassed. The important thing to remember is that these are all normal emotions and they'll soon fade away. Before long, chatting to a professional will feel no different from visiting the local garage to get the car looked at, though rather than having your engine fine-tuned, it'll be your brain – and after a while you'll feel all the better for it.

TACTICAL BRIEFING: THERAPY – WHAT YOU NEED TO KNOW

FINDING A THERAPIST IS LIKE BUYING A SUIT

Yes, you can buy one off the peg, but the cut might not be quite right. In much the same way that you want to attend a fancy do looking your absolute best, you should get a therapist that fits you perfectly, so don't feel bad about shopping around if that's an option for you. My own first few experiences of therapy were horrendous. I sat in a succession of stale, soulless offices, facing a person behind a desk. I think I saw the same shitty pictures hanging on the wall in each place; there was a copy of the *National Geographic* in every waiting room, too. I often came away feeling like I was in the wrong place with the wrong person.

It was only once I'd met my long-term therapist, Alex Lagaisse, that I began to experience any tangible, positive change. Alex recognized that I had lived a large chunk of my life outdoors, while working in extreme environments, and she asked if I would feel more comfortable conducting our chats away from the office. I agreed, and every week we walked and talked in the woods, me laying out what had happened, her listening. I soon found that being in nature helped me to open up because it was a setting I was well adapted to. Your personality might require something altogether different, though. It could be that you want to sit on a park bench. Maybe you like the office environment, or perhaps you'd prefer to conduct your sessions over the phone, or on Zoom. There's only one way to do therapy, and that's in the style that suits *you*.

REMEMBER: TURN THE NEGATIVES INTO A POSITIVE

As I've mentioned elsewhere, it's vital you turn the negative elements of a situation into positives, and therapy is the perfect environment in which to test this theory. Yes, you'll feel weird. Yes, you're going to have to open up to a stranger. And yes, you'll need to get vulnerable with someone you've never met before. All of those things are enough to send someone into a bit of a spiral. But, if you can treat these experiences as stages in a journey, there's a strong chance that the first session will feel less overwhelming. To reach that point, try thinking about the following:

- You might be meeting the person who can get you back on track.
- You're going to find out a lot about yourself.
- You're going to become a better version of you.

Even if your first few experiences with therapy have felt bad, that's OK, too. I often get messages from people going, 'Oh, I tried to speak to a professional, but it was shit. I can't be bothered going through that again.' I get the frustration, but it's the wrong attitude. Instead it helps to think of the bad sessions as lessons. You've discovered that a particular therapist wasn't the right fit for you, and you know more about what you *don't* want from a therapist. That's as important as knowing what you *do* want.

GO AT YOUR OWN PACE

While I fully advocate ripping off the Band-Aid and asking for help, how you explain your situation to a counsellor is a personal choice. It might be that you feel comfortable laying it all out in the very first sitting, or it might be that it takes you weeks, even months, to get there. In my case, I decided to treat what was going on in my head like an injury. When I recently broke my leg, my attitude was that I wouldn't get any better by faffing about. Instead I had to allow the surgeons to cut me open so they could see everything inside and figure out how to patch me up. I felt the same way about therapy, but that's just me. How you approach this point is your decision and a professional will help you to get there. And if you cry, don't feel bad about it. It's a natural reaction. The fact that you're comfortable with being emotionally vulnerable should be celebrated rather than covered up.

→ THE LOOK FORWARD

Take charge of your recovery. *Today.* But after that, therapy is something that should happen at your pace, so find a speed you're comfy with, whether that's with the frequency of your sessions, the way in which you open up, or how you chat to other people about your situation. The world is in the middle of a mental health crisis at the moment and too many people are dying by suicide rather than seeking the help they need. Chatting to someone is often the first step to recovery, so make it your priority.

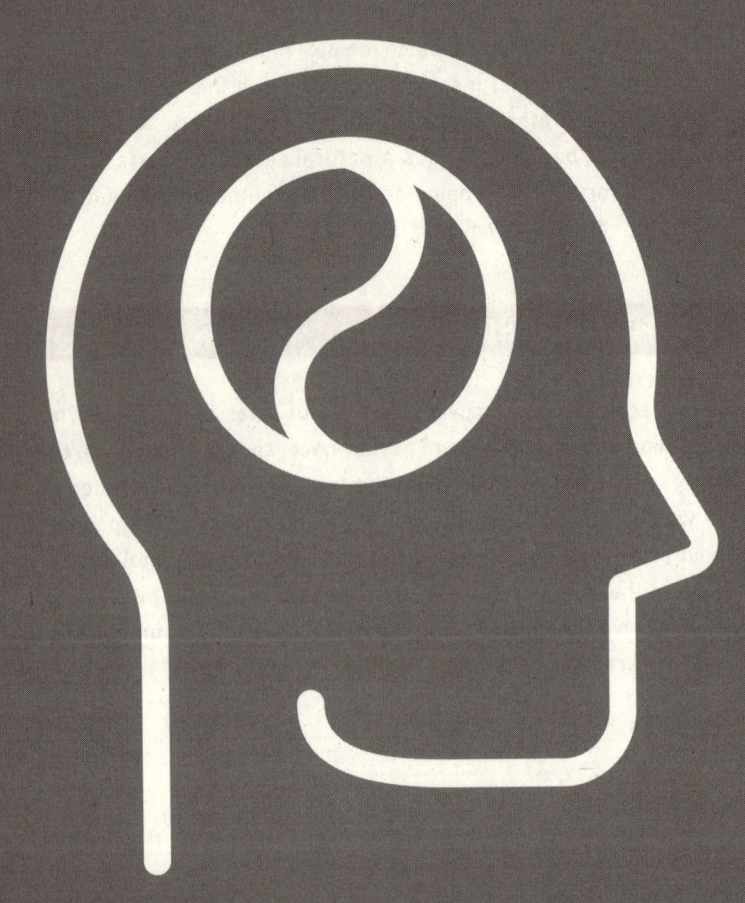

PART FOUR:
CALM

INTRODUCTION

Moments of calm are a rare gift. Within them an individual can reflect and grow by analysing their previous performances and establishing new strategies for improvement. These lulls are also opportunities for learning, and in periods of inactivity it's important that a person upskills, establishes new and productive routines, and reaffirms their plans and priorities.

The problem for many people, including me, is that calm can sometimes be hard to identify – we often mistake stillness for boredom, underemployment or loneliness. A good example of this is the twilight zone that takes place between Christmas and New Year. In these situations, we fill the calm (and opportunity) with unproductive activities and FOMO. As a consequence, we're left feeling underprepared or off-guard when a new mission comes along or chaos kicks in once more.

In the military elite, the importance of maximizing the quiet moments between operations and tours has been long recognized. Whenever I returned home to the UK, my group would usually be sent on training courses so that our education could continue. This ensured we remained several steps ahead of the enemy. We also took time to analyse our recent activities through intelligence briefings, where we shared our conclusions with lads who were preparing to head into the thick of it ahead of us. This was an effective way for the British Armed Forces to strengthen its armour as a whole.

These days I follow a similar pattern whenever I come away from an expedition or a filming trip with *SAS: Who Dares Wins*. In the first few days after my return there's a temptation to immediately fall back into my usual routines so that I can reclaim

a sense of familiarity and comfort. As discussed in Part Two, Chapter 5, experience has taught me that I should sit back and relax, sometimes literally, in order to maximize what is always a brief moment of calm. So instead I'll reset my routines in order to reach full strength by the time the work cranks up again: I like to learn new skills and build positive habits that will improve upon the ones I had before; I'll also work on my support network, and dream and plan for my next mission.

As my work in the military elite has taught me, moments of calm are incredibly rare. When they do arrive, it helps to be fully prepared and eager to engage, so that you can grow stronger and upskill in new ways. The following lessons should help you to maximize any opportunities that arise.

CHAPTER 1
ROUTINE-BUILDING

I'm a believer that routine is everything. During my time in the Royal Marines I was able to thrive under extreme pressure because my day was mapped out and my procedures and duties were fixed in place. That created a sense of stability. Later, too, when I was serving as an elite operator at home in the UK, I knew where I had to be and when, and what was expected of me, at all times. Unsurprisingly, this feeling of structure was much harder to maintain in war, so I made sure to install a series of small routines into my day. For example, when stationed in a desert base, I trained in the gym whenever possible; I then showed up for work, grabbed a coffee and prepped for the day's operations. As I moved from mission to mission, switching from the relative security and comforts of base life to the stresses of violent action, these small events helped to keep me grounded.

Having eventually sorted my head out, and found a period of relative calm after my military career had ended, I anchored myself to a new routine of tasks based on the following:

- Exercise and nutrition: I trained every day, and I planned my meals and stuck to a regime of clean eating.
- Health and well-being: Taking cold showers, spending time outdoors and dynamically meditating

(see Part Three, Chapter 3) kept me in a good place.
- Brotherhood: I spent time with mates, which acted as a healthy pressure valve.
- Purpose: I found a sense of satisfaction by focusing my mind on work projects and expeditions while helping people with similar mental health experiences to mine.

Routine-building had been a major part of my old career; I just hadn't realized it could work equally well in an everyday setting. The same applied to being psychologically flexible, as I had been in war, so I adapted my routines for a variety of situations. These days, I perform a set of processes when I'm at home, but that timetable changes slightly if I'm working abroad in an unfamiliar location. In these scenarios, my preferred routines shift depending on my commitments, but I make sure to always focus on the key areas that are most important to me: exercise and nutrition, health and well-being, brotherhood and purpose. Hitting these categories in some way helps me to rest easy at night, whereas my head feels like it's on fire if I don't.

Here's the lesson: once a person plans out a series of solid routines during a period of calm, they will act like points of cover and an individual can find shelter within them. My structure is as follows:

- The gym session = stability.
- The morning cold shower = stability.
- The check-in with mates = stability.
- The expedition-planning sessions = stability.

In my case, these daily activities allow me to function effectively, whether that's on an expedition, a risky work trip or even a long stint away from home. That's because I know there's a safe place to retreat to if things get manic. This is the reason why everyone should have a schedule of activities to fall back upon in times of chaos – though the only place to plan one is during a period of calm: I've learned the hard way that trying to figure this stuff out when your life has turned to rat shit only adds to the pain.

TACTICAL BRIEFING: UNDERSTANDING TIME APPRECIATION

While I was serving in the Royal Marines, the concept of routine-building was instilled subtly rather than being explicitly explained to me. When I first joined, I can remember being told the importance of washing upon waking up and washing before going to bed. Apart from that, it was down to me to figure out how to organize everything that needed to happen in between, such as when to prepare my uniform and how to arrive at training on time. For the first three months, my life in Basic Training was a nightmare. I often got up at 3 a.m. to iron my shirts and perfect my kit husbandry, because my routine was all over the shop.

That all changed once I'd developed a keener understanding of 'time appreciation'. In operational terms, this was a concept in which a mission began at a set time known as H-Hour. For the job to run smoothly, each task or process that needed to take place beforehand was then figured out, with timings for each one, such as kit preparation and our walk towards the target we were attacking. By working backwards from H-Hour, a timetable of events was established:

- **Step One:** H-Hour is 03:00 hours. *That's when we'll hit the enemy.*
- **Step Two:** How long will it take to walk on to target? *Two hours. We'll set out at 01:00 hours.*

- **Step Three:** How long will the group need to square away their kit? *One hour. This process starts no later than midnight.*
- **Step Four:** A set of orders takes two hours. *We'll begin that at 22:00.*

And so on.

Handily, running a time-appreciation check will often expose the poorly functioning areas in a person's routines. In the above example, it might be that the orders process runs over on a regular basis, impacting the time allotted to kit prep, in which case adjustments need to be made. So, do yourself a favour and run a time-appreciation check on your daily commitments. A good starting point would be the commute to work: try setting your ideal arrival time (H-Hour) and work backwards from there, establishing how long it takes to execute your morning routine. You'll notice how almost insignificant moments, such as prepping and eating breakfast, and packing the work bag, can affect your overall goal.

→ THE LOOK FORWARD

When building a routine it's important to identify the targets you want to hit. My personal list comprises exercise and nutrition, health and well-being, brotherhood and purpose, but you might require something very different. List the things that are most important to you and figure out how to work them into your daily schedule.

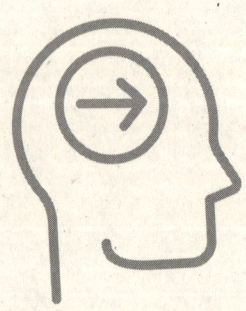

CHAPTER 2
OWN THE
MORNING

This is going to sound like rubbish, but it's not hard to feel great in the morning. All it takes is the execution of a series of easy tasks and routines that can be quickly ticked off, in order, before the day starts for real. Meditation, a burst of exercise and getting a dose of morning sun: it's claimed that executing these small, simple tasks can make a massive psychological difference to a person's emotional well-being, because they create structure, hold us to a high standard and set the tone for the rest of the day. Just completing these jobs can be enough to remind us that we're open for business, regardless of what that business might be. Furthermore, ticking off a series of set activities on a daily basis gives us a stable platform from which to work, even in times of chaos.

Below is an outline of my morning routine whenever I'm at home. I devised this list in a moment of calm, as you should do. And obviously it changes if I'm working away or on an expedition, though whenever I'm on those trips I'll still have a daily list of tasks I like to focus on before my day begins. As with some of the other activities I've suggested in these pages, developing a morning routine is a completely personal process; owing to all sorts of variables, such as your job, family status, health, etc., what works for me may not necessarily be a great fit for you, and vice versa. However, there are one or two things I'm going to recommend you do to power up your day and I'll highlight them as we go.

THE FIRST FIVE MINUTES

The alarm goes off. Rather than hitting the snooze button, I make a point of sitting at the end of my bed for five minutes in order to run an emotional stocktake. (See Part Two, Chapters 7 and 8.) I'm really only asking myself one question: *How am I feeling?* From there I'll figure out what I should do in order to maximize that emotion (if it's positive) or minimize it (if it's not). This should be an integral part of everyone's day.

A LITTLE DISCOMFORT

Once I've spent five minutes getting my head straight, I take a cold shower. The process charges me up with adrenaline and I feel ready to get stuck into the day. Again, this is a non-negotiable part of the morning for me. As you'll discover in the next chapter, it should be for you too. No excuses.

SELF-CARE

I'm a stickler for moisturizing my face and I do it regularly, not because I'm obsessed with my wrinkles but because I was taught in the military that self-care was an important process when functioning in extreme environments. If I didn't dry my feet in the jungle, I'd succumb to footrot. If I didn't treat my blisters before a series of gruelling time tests across the Brecon Beacons, I'd become incapacitated. Some people take the piss out of me for it, but as far as I'm concerned, it's a psychological cue rather than an act of vanity. If I don't look after myself and I start falling apart, my work does too.

BREAKFAST

I try to eat breakfast every day. I'll have a bowl of porridge, though every now and then I treat myself to a plate of pancakes or waffles.

TRAINING

I'm lucky. Physical exercise is a part of my job and I'm expected to be in good condition in order to function effectively on *SAS: Who Dares Wins* and the other TV productions I work on. The timings on my gym sessions vary. I might crack on at 06:00; sometimes I leave it a little later and head in at 09:00. The important thing is that I push myself for a couple of hours every day. I wouldn't be able to do my job without a high standard of physical and mental fitness.

TACTICAL BRIEFING: GRATITUDE IS A TOOL

Not so long ago, I checked in on a mate who had been having a rough time. As we talked through his day he told me he'd been practising gratitude in the morning. Apparently it was having a positive impact on his mental well-being.

It wasn't a technique I was familiar with.

'What do you mean by that?' I said.

'Well, I wake up in the morning and spend five to ten minutes listing the things I'm happy for in life,' he said. 'My wife, kids, business, mates . . . It puts me in a cracking mood. You should try it.'

At first I wasn't so sure; it sounded a bit happy-clappy. But the following morning, once the alarm had gone off and I'd run through my emotional scan, I thought of a list of things I was thankful for.

In this case, I considered my relationship, my family life, a good bill of health and a career that gave me purpose. My mate had been right. It *was* pretty hard for me to feel shitty after checking in on some of the good things I had going on in life. Since then, I've made a few minutes of gratitude a part of my morning routine. I've been through some rough times in the past couple of years, but whenever things have looked bleak, I've been able to bring some semblance of positivity by reminding myself that, at the very least, I've got people who love me and a roof over my head. That's sometimes been enough to get me through a shitty day.

⊙ THE LOOK FORWARD

Focus in on your morning routine and introduce some positive processes that will set your head straight for the day. These will act as anchors to balance you whenever chaos strikes. And don't skip the non-negotiables. You'll thank me for them later.

CHAPTER 3
TAKE A COLD PLUNGE

I have an interesting relationship with cold water. For the best part of ten years I jumped in and out of it as a combat diver and I bloody hated the icy blast that ripped through me whenever I was dunked into a churning sea. Then, at the beginning of 2021, two interesting conversations happened. The first was with a mate who had recently fallen into the habit of taking cold showers in the evening. Apparently, they helped him to sleep better. The second chat was with Wim Hof, the extreme athlete mentioned earlier in the book. Nicknamed 'The Iceman', he had created the Wim Hof Method, which brought together meditation, cold-temperature exposure and various breathing techniques. Through a combination of all three, Wim had managed to run the fastest half-marathon on ice and snow while barefoot in 2007. He had also established a world record for the longest swim under ice, without flippers or a specially designed suit, managing a distance of 57.5 metres. (This record was later extended to 80.99 metres in 2021 by David Vencl from the Czech Republic.)

Unsurprisingly, Wim was a bit of a wild card when I first spoke to him during a podcast interview. He told me, 'First of all, take the cold shower, every day.'

'Yeah?'

'Yeah! I always say, "A cold shower a day keeps the doctor away." You just do it – keep it simple. I could write a whole book on the cold shower . . . The investment to go into the cold shower is the best thing you can do in your life, to yourself. *Take the damn cold shower every day.* The energy is coming. Stress goes away. Your vascular system is being optimized, the way nature meant it to be.'

Wim wasn't kidding. *He wanted me to make the cold shower a part of my day.* So I did, and I'm currently having two daily – one in the morning and one before I go to bed – and it's become a ritual, like cleaning my teeth or making a coffee first thing. Don't get me wrong: it was bloody horrible at first. When I began the experiment, my fitness regime involved a lot of training on a static bike and after every session I jumped into an ice-cold bath, which was a miserable experience. Then I moved on to the shower, and I would stand there, shivering my bollocks off for two or three minutes, but the impact was undeniable. My mood lifted. I felt energized throughout the day. And I slept like a baby. The jury is still out on whether the process is a placebo or not, but as long as it's working for me, I'll carry on doing it, while passing on Wim's words of wisdom to you:

Take the damn cold shower every day.

TACTICAL BRIEFING: UNDERSTANDING THE SCIENCE

Before standing in the shower and contemplating whether to go for hot or cold, consider the following:

REASON ONE: IT'S SUGGESTED THAT COLD SHOWERS MIGHT HELP WITH DEPRESSION

Some limited studies have determined that people who took cold showers over a period of several months experienced an upswing in mood. Reportedly, the cold triggered an increase of beta-endorphin and noradrenaline into the blood. Beta-endorphin decreases bodily stress and helps with pain management and behavioural stability; noradrenaline is a chemical that keeps us alert and gives us more energy. (Too much of it causes anxiety; too little and we get depressed.) It's also argued that the cold receptors in the body, which are found on the skin, bombard the brain with electrical impulses to create an 'anti-depressive' effect during an icy shower or bath. There are two important points to note, however: 1) these studies have recommended that more research is needed, and 2) don't take a cold shower if you have a heart condition or other serious health conditions.

REASON TWO: THERE'S SOME EVIDENCE THAT COLD-WATER EXPOSURE HELPS WITH OUR METABOLISM

It's currently believed that our metabolism is being boosted as the body fights to reach a comfortable temperature when in cold water, a process which burns calories. Just don't expect to shiver your way to a shredded body. When it comes to fitness, exercise and a good nutrition plan still does most of the heavy lifting.

REASON THREE: WE BECOME MORE ALERT

Here's some anecdotal evidence. Stepping into a cold shower gives me a surge of adrenaline, but there are other physical changes going on: my breathing quickens, I can feel my heart pounding, and my blood pressure increases. This makes me feel more alert and gives me a kick up the arse if my morning training session seems unappealing.

⊖ THE LOOK FORWARD

Don't expect to enjoy the experience of jumping into your first Baltic-cold shower. It'll be a horror show. Instead, approach the process gradually by taking your shower as per usual and then, at the end, cranking up the cold. Initially your body will freak out, but hang in there and begin a countdown in your head. Try to last for 45–60 seconds on the first go and then build yourself up each time until you can manage a full three minutes, at which point you'll be as nails as Wim Hof.

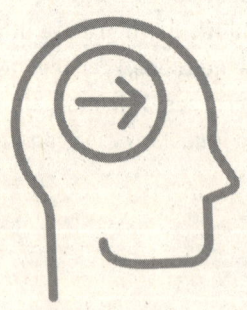

CHAPTER 4
WEAPONIZE YOUR CIRCADIAN RHYTHMS

Scientific fact: taking control of the body's circadian rhythms during a period of calm can help an individual to function effectively when life turns kinetic again. *We sleep well; we recover well; we perform well.* But if hardwiring our internal clock sounds complicated, it might help to first dig into what circadian rhythms *are* and what they actually *do*.

THE CIRCADIAN RHYTHM CYCLE

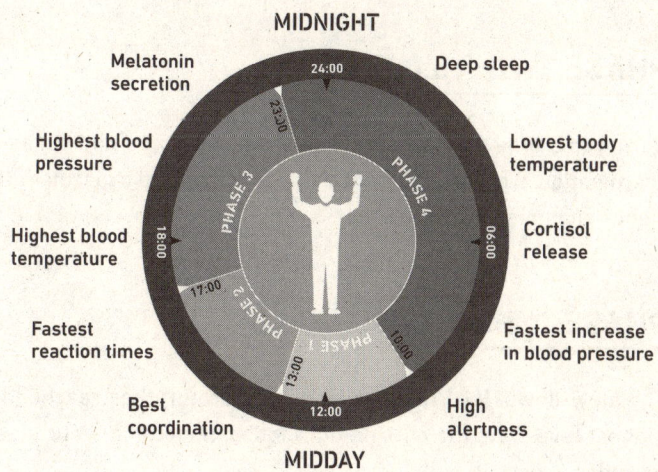

MIDNIGHT

Melatonin secretion

Deep sleep

Highest blood pressure

Lowest body temperature

Highest blood temperature

Cortisol release

Fastest reaction times

Fastest increase in blood pressure

Best coordination

High alertness

MIDDAY

24:00 · 23:30 · PHASE 3 · PHASE 4 · 18:00 · 06:00 · 17:00 · PHASE 2 · PHASE 1 · 08:00 · 13:00 · 12:00

According to America's National Institute of General Medical Sciences, 'Circadian rhythms are physical, mental, and behavioural changes that follow a 24-hour cycle. These natural processes respond primarily to light and dark and affect most living things, including animals, plants, and microbes . . . One example of a light-related circadian rhythm is sleeping at night and being awake during the day.'

It's for this reason that the effort required to nail a good night's kip begins from the minute you wake up, rather than the minute you turn the light off at night. It's also why our energy levels spike and crash throughout the day in four key phases:

PHASE ONE: 10:00–13:00

The sweet spot. We're fully awake during this time because our body temperature is rising. We feel sharp and energetic, and our alertness is on point. The morning is my preferred time for training, partly for this reason.

PHASE TWO: 13:00–17:00

During this time we have our fastest reaction time and our best coordination. We also experience a peak in our cardiovascular efficiency and muscular strength.

PHASE THREE: 17:00–23:00

The slow-down. By 19:00 our body temperature has reached its highest levels. As the outside light fades, melatonin – our sleep hormone – kicks in.

PHASE FOUR: 23:00–10:00

Time to sleep. While we're snoring, we move from restorative sleep to deep sleep, and then to REM sleep, until our melatonin release stops, at around 06:00. Although we might wake up anywhere between 05:00 and 08:00, an adult won't feel like they're firing on all cylinders until around 09:00.

Sadly, so much of what we do during the day screws with our circadian rhythms, which then prevents us from hitting our peak levels and resting efficiently. We drink caffeine and energy drinks, or eat chocolate for a burst of power, only to crash an hour or so afterwards. We spend way too much time staring at our blue-light devices, such as laptops and smartphones, which are known to suppress the body's melatonin release. As a result of these habits we become overstimulated and find it difficult to sleep. The following morning we feel knackered, so we return to caffeine, sugar and social media as a way of dragging ourselves through the day. Then the process repeats itself all over again.

The good news is that it's possible to implement one or two strategies in order to maintain our circadian rhythms and bring some balance to our energy levels during the day. The first of these requires us to take in a healthy dose of morning sunlight within an hour of waking. Our eyes are receptors for the brain (some cells on the back of our eyes actually *are* brain) and they assist in regulating our internal clocks. By exposing them to a dose of morning sunlight, you'll set a timer telling the brain to slow down around sixteen hours later.

The second tactic is the setting of a relaxing and productive evening routine – one that's every bit as detailed as our morning schedule. This can help us to slow down and to rest the mind. In my case, I'll stop looking at my phone at around 21:00. I then plan out the next day's events, writing down my goals and squaring away any kit if I need to. Before I go to bed, I'll take another cold shower, dry my hair, brush my teeth and drink a cup of camomile tea. Then I'll read for five to ten minutes. Before long my eyes are drooping and I'm turning off the lights. I sound like an old man, I know, but as a routine it delivers every time.

TACTICAL BRIEFING: UNWIND LIKE AN ELITE OPERATOR

Planning a sleep schedule during a military tour is impossible. Operations often happen in the dead of night, and I remember a lot of the time we'd be called out with zero warning. However, when working back in the UK, the higher-ups often encouraged us to rest in an efficient manner, but there was very little intel on how to actually do so. That's all changed. These days there are performance manuals for those men and women currently employed by the British Armed Forces, and within them there's often a series of tips on how to prepare for a good night's kip. Suggestions include:

- Set the room you're sleeping in to the ideal temperature of 18°C.
- Darken the room.
- No blue light one hour before sleeping.
- Understand that booze will impact your sleep quality.
- Make your sleeping space a stress-free zone. No TV, no laptops, no video games. Use earplugs if it's noisy, or an eye mask if there's regular disruption in the house, such as other people turning on the lights at weird hours.

If you're in any doubt as to the importance of maintaining a healthy circadian rhythm, research has shown that 'jet-lagged' rats, with desynchronized internal clocks, display signs of anxiety and depression. There's also evidence to suggest that a chaotic circadian rhythm can lead to an increase in cancer risks, heart disease and even poor dental health.

→ THE LOOK FORWARD

Within an hour of waking up, step into the sunlight. Stand there for ten minutes on a sunny day, or for twenty minutes when it's cloudy. If it's cold or raining, wrap up and use an umbrella. Don't wear sunglasses and don't stare directly at the sun. Make this process a part of your daily routine.

CHAPTER 5
UNDERSTANDING GROUNDRUSH

When I was in the military, the term 'groundrush' was used to describe the illusory, unsettling moment during every parachute jump when the terrain seemed to lurch up at terrifying speeds towards the commando as they approached it. For the inexperienced, this sensation came as a shock – even though it was an inevitable conclusion to every landing – because everything that preceded it was so ridiculously calming and serene. One minute you were floating gently down to earth, taking in the scenery about you; the next the ground was rushing up at a million miles per hour, even though the air speed hadn't changed in the slightest.

During training, the first few minutes of my early jumps always followed the same pattern: 1) I'd make the stressful leap from the plane, adopt my freefall position for a set period of time, and then sigh with relief as my canopy billowed open; 2) From a position of several thousand metres up, I'd soar through the air like a bird . . . until 3) *Shit! Shit! Shit!* The landing zone, which had once been a dot in the distance, rushed into view. In those moments it felt like I was plummeting to the deck like a lead weight.

That was groundrush.

Since leaving the military, it's become a term I've used to describe the frantic weeks, days and hours before every deadline in my work and personal life. Examples have included:

- The always-painful tax returns deadline.
- The final twenty-four hours of packing and prepping before a work trip.
- The last few days when planning a stag or hen do.

Groundrush in these situations is unavoidable. Anything with a hard stop will come at you fast, because you never have as much time as you think in life, whether you're dropping out of the sky or planning a home renovation. But if, during moments of calm, you can master the art of prepping the final stages of a project in advance, you'll soon be able to avoid any stress during periods of chaos.

Here's how you do and *don't* manage it.

TACTICAL BRIEFING: THE FALSE DEADLINE ALTERNATIVE

There's a major misconception in modern business that ground-rush can be avoided with a false deadline. Sadly, that's bollocks. Yes, it can be a handy resource if you have a friend, teammate or significant other who is habitually late: if you're leaving together for an important engagement, giving them a departure time that's fifteen minutes earlier than necessary can almost guarantee that *you* won't run late even if *they* do. However, when it comes to establishing deadlines in a work or team environment, false deadlines are often counterproductive. The truth is that they'll usually work at first. But if a team has been mugged off once, they're unlikely to fall for the same trick a second time and any sense of loyalty and morale will crumble. Meanwhile, when setting a *personal* false deadline, there's no real consequence from failure. How can there be when, in truth, the individual knows there's more time for them to work if things go south?

My answer when establishing the ending of a project has been to establish a series of tactical 'mini-deadlines' that lead up to a hard stop – a list of tasks that can be nailed in increments over a period of weeks or days, rather than in a mad flap at the end. A good case study for this would be the build-up to a holiday abroad. In theory, this should be a time of optimism and excitement – vacations are usually a reward for toughing out a year of hard work and a chance to unwind and recharge. Instead, they often become a pain in the arse, especially in the days leading up to departure. Plane tickets need to be double-checked, and there are cabs to book and clothes to buy. Some tropical countries require vaccinations; others want tourist visas. Then there's the pain of last-minute packing. Instead of being a fun experience, the days leading up to a break can be more annoying than the events that motivated a person to book one in the first place.

Instead, why not establish a list of the tasks that need to be done in advance, with deadlines, and establish a penalty for failing to execute them on time? My advice would be to knock off the really stressful jobs first, like checking your passport expiry dates and filling in any required paperwork. If you fail to complete a task, a penalty should be incurred, such as the cancellation of a social event. Ask your travelling companions to hold you accountable if you're not a hard taskmaster.

⊕ THE LOOK FORWARD

In times of calm, get into the habit of seeing off groundrush. You can practise for this by building a timetable of mini-tasks for yourself in advance of a fun, flexible deadline, such as a weekend trip away. By the time you get to a more chaotic situation, you should have gathered the necessary experience of what, and what not, to do.

CHAPTER 6
FIND THE
RIGHT PERSON

I struggled throughout the first eighteen weeks of Royal Marines Basic Training. I wasn't a total knob-end – in fact I was physically on point most of the time – but I hadn't yet learned how to manage the smaller but no less important details of the job, such as kit husbandry and personal admin. After failing to make the grade by the midway point, it was decided by the higher-ups that I should be 'backtrooped', a process whereby a recruit is put back into the intake behind theirs so they can master the skills that previously passed them by. Part of this rigmarole involved joining up with Hunter Troop (now known as Hunter Company), which was a group comprising recruits who were carrying injuries, or who had professional failures, and had failed a crucial test. Members of Hunter Troop were usually conducting remedial physical training, remedial lectures, and on the odd occasion assisting in training exercises where they would play the enemy or the walking wounded. Some, but not all of the recruits, were reasonably experienced and knew how to play the game.

At first being backtrooped felt like a pain in the hoop, but thank God it happened, because I was immediately introduced to an instructor who helped to turn me around. The guy was a Falklands vet, but unlike some of the older soldiers I'd met from that conflict, he wasn't a jaded, horrible fucker who enjoyed beasting inexperienced recruits. Instead, he wanted to share his knowledge with the younger lads so they could fulfil their potential.

Early on in the phase, he told me, 'Right, we're going out on an exercise and I'm going to show you how to be a soldier.'

He wasn't kidding. Over the course of a few weeks I was taught the finer details of field craft, plus a series of skills I probably wouldn't have learned otherwise, because much of Basic Training seemed to be happening in a whirlwind and there was barely enough time to think.

At one point I remember him showing me how to plant my feet as I moved.

'When you're approaching a target, think about rolling your feet down on to the floor,' he said, 'from heel to ball – to reduce the noise.'

I hadn't even considered the technique before. He later taught me the finer art of scaling obstacle crossings, before detailing the mindset required to slow a situation down when being bumped by the enemy. I loved it.

Because I wasn't being assessed at the time, I felt zero pressure and soon came to terms with the flaws in my techniques that had caused me to fail a few weeks previously. I also upped my game in the areas in which I was already excelling. Most importantly, the guy talked to me like a proper human being, rather than a useless sack of shit, and I thrived. By the time I returned to Recruit training, I had grown immeasurably and I passed the course, finishing as one of the better lads in the group. And all because I'd found the right person at exactly the right time.

TACTICAL BRIEFING: FIND YOUR MENTOR

All of us need some assistance from time to time, no matter how strong or capable we think we are. For example, you won't see a stacked weightlifter trying to smash their personal bests in the gym without some assistance. He or she will always have one other with them so they can 'spot' the bar should things go askew. This help is invaluable – nobody wants to suffer crushed ribs or a damaged larynx due to a falling, overloaded bench press. But weirdly, when it comes to the psychological or tactical challenges in life, so few of us will admit to needing assistance. That's because we're proud, and asking for help can be a real dent to the ego.

As I've learned, the right mentor can be a game-changer – and the best time to seek one out is in a period of calm, when time is on your side. (Though there's nothing to stop you finding an 'emergency mentor' in times of chaos.) Without the assistance of my backtroop instructor, my life would probably look very different today. There's a chance I might not have passed Basic Training, and consequently I would never have made it into the military elite, or into a career on the telly. *The lesson?* If a mentor (or some other helpful individual) can turn around the fortunes of a sixteen-year-old sprog, as I was back then, then they can work for you too. You only have to connect with the right person.

There's no set procedure for making this happen, sadly. It's a game of instinct, but you'll definitely know the individual once you've found them. To ensure you're not simply making do with the first contact you meet, consider the following questions:

- **Do you feel good when you speak to this person?**
- **Do you feel comfortable?**
- **Do you like being around them?**
- **Are they helping?**

If the answer is 'no' to any of the questions, then move on to the next person.

Sometimes the positive connection can happen immediately. Picture someone recovering from a major operation. A way for them to find the right person would be to contact a friend or family member who's experienced a similar process. If that isn't possible, there are usually support groups that can offer emotional and practical assistance with rehabilitation, doctor discussions or coping mechanisms. This same approach can be applied to all sorts of scenarios, including bankruptcy, entrepreneurship, immigration, legal issues, bereavement, career advancement and education. All that's required of you is to be open to the idea of talking to someone about your situation.

If that feels intimidating, then practise for the experience by just casting the net. A good way to do this is to familiarize yourself with the practice of chatting to strangers. One technique I've recently employed when mastering this skill is to make a point of talking to at least one random person a day. The connection can happen anywhere. It might be on a bus, in the newsagent or at the gym, but the rules are straightforward:

1) I pick a person.
2) I spark up a conversation.
3) I attempt to make them laugh.

It's a great way of building up the confidence to seek out a mentor, support group or to simply expand your social circle.

If you're of the opinion that you're not currently in need of a mentor, maybe advance your portfolio of skills by becoming one yourself, because the benefits are huge. I recently delivered a talk to the instructors at Commando Training Centre Royal Marines at Lympstone in Devon, where I recounted my positive experience in Hunter Troop.

'Whether you like it or not, for a short period of time you will be the single most influential person in the lives of these Potential Royal Marines Commandos,' I said. 'You might call them the bottom-feeders, but if you can find out what those bottom-feeders like eating, you'll probably make good Marines out of them. And even if you don't, your efforts might result in them taking away some life-defining skills that they'll utilize later on. Your role means that you'll make an impression on them – good or bad. So do you want to be remembered for being a positive force or a negative one?'

Consider this statement if someone ever leans on you for advice, because not only will the experience likely be rewarding and educational, but it might advance your own ambitions, should the person in question become a force of their own later down the line.

⊙ THE LOOK FORWARD

Build your own Directing Staff. By that I don't mean you should corral a group of grizzled ball-breakers into screaming at you whenever the mood takes them. Instead, pick a few key areas in your life that need a little work. Examples might include personal finances, health and fitness, communication skills or stress management. Then contact someone you know with a background in each category (or reach out for help in the professional sector) and ask if you can lean on them for advice from time to time.

CHAPTER 7
TAKE THE OPPORTUNITY TO UPSKILL

We called it the 'Wolverine's Lair': a section of the base's gym in which the lads from my group worked on their close-combat fighting skills: boxing, Brazilian jiu-jitsu, wrestling and Muay Thai – we did the lot. But this wasn't a random mishmash of blokes kicking the crap out of one another for fun. Instead, each one of us had taken on the challenge of learning a different combat sport because, firstly, the work helped us to stay in shape (it also added novelty in times when our regular training schedules might have felt a bit stale), and, secondly, because it gave each of us a new way of taking down the enemy in situations when a weapon might not have been employable.

The 'Wednesday Night Lair Session' soon became a weekly event in which everyone practised their latest moves as we punched, blocked, kicked and rolled around for a few hours. It was great fun. One of the lads was a big lump and turned out to be a very handy wrestler. Another was an expert in Brazilian jiu-jitsu and showed us the best techniques for hand-to-hand scrapping. At the end of the evening, everyone jumped into a big tear-up and from a distance it must have looked like a mass brawl – probably because it was. In the end, our commanding officer banned the Wednesday night sessions because a higher percentage of operators were injuring themselves in the Wolverine's Lair than they were during missions.

I loved the experience, because it meant that I was upskilling and adding new weapons to my armoury. And my learning wasn't just restricted to close combat and martial arts. Whenever I returned to the UK after a military tour, I was dispatched to all sorts of courses so that I could research the latest developments in surveillance, optical tech and weapons systems; I travelled around the country (and abroad) to pick up new techniques in performance driving (for high-speed pursuits), interrogation and intelligence gathering, which was handy when it came to keeping up with the latest challenges in cyber warfare. Some of the courses I was attending felt like abstract choices at the time. (I can't tell you what they were, out of respect for the practices of the group.) However, once I was inserted back into action, they usually made a lot of sense.

Put together, all of these techniques helped to sharpen my game. They also increased my value in the battlespace. But upskilling in this way isn't a process confined to the military elite; it's an easily applicable process we should all employ if we're to grow as individuals.

TACTICAL BRIEFING: DON'T STOP LEARNING

When we fail to learn new skills, we stagnate, no matter our profession or lifestyle. The sports physio needs to learn new massage techniques. The architect needs to keep up with the latest advancements in design. And the tax adviser needs to understand the latest changes in the law. Then there are the benefits to our physical and mental health. Studies have shown that becoming upskilled in a group setting can improve our social lives. It should also go without saying that increasing our repertoire of talents makes us more valuable to employers, which can then lead to an uptick in our financial fortunes – being the most on-the-ball individual in the team increases the odds of a pay rise or promotion.

TAKE THE OPPORTUNITY TO UPSKILL

Really there's no excuse not to carry on learning beyond our school, college and university years. I see people that haven't taken on those challenges and they tend to be either bored, because they're not pushing themselves out of the comfort zone, or frustrated, having not fulfilled their potential. It's for this reason that I'm always working to improve, usually in the area of fitness (because it's my job) but also in communication. As I mentioned earlier in Part Two, Chapter 9, I've learned several new breathing techniques so that I can improve my delivery during speaking gigs. But I've also picked up new skills for when I need to give advice while working in the mental health industry, or when I'm dishing out direction, instruction and encouragement in a team setting. In those situations it's important I get myself across clearly.

By churning through books and documentaries, and chatting to experts in the field, I eventually hope to become a master of communication. But the work is a constant process. Even if I'm out for the evening, I'm constantly thinking about how to present myself in a public setting. Everyone's different so everyone needs to be communicated to according to personality type, and whenever I come away from a conversation with a new person I'll analyse the chat. I ask myself questions: *Did I listen enough? Or did I butt in every now and then?* Then I'll spend some time going through a book on the subject, or watching a YouTube video, so I can improve in that area. (As an aside, I'd also like to do a degree in anthropology, and I'm trying to read as many books on people and places as I can. Finding the time for such an undertaking will be a bit tricky, given my work schedule, but I'm determined to look into the idea during my next period of calm.)

The idea of improving my communication skills might seem a rudimentary example, but that's exactly the point. No matter what we're doing, there's always room for improvement and, as the military elite have shown, over and over, there's a tactical benefit to adopting new techniques and adapting to change. Keeping on top of the skills you already have is one thing. Taking them to the next level will ensure you're always one step ahead of the competition, or enemy. So, maximize your moments of calm by signing up for a course, either online or in person, or reading the latest research in your field. Watch a YouTube tutorial on a subject you're interested in. Doing so will guarantee you remain fixed at the sharp end of the action.

⊙ THE LOOK FORWARD

Develop your own Wolverine's Lair. But before the fists start flying, I don't mean you should create a twenty-first-century version of *Fight Club*. Instead, if you're in a team setting I'd like you to delegate a new skill to each member of your group. Then encourage them to build their learning in that area, while sharing any techniques or tactics that might help the collective as a whole. This process also works if you're flying solo; you just have to pick an avenue of learning that will assist you in the long run.

CHAPTER 8
NUTRITION = ARMOUR

Focusing on your nutrition is next to impossible in war. When I was in the military elite, there usually wasn't the time to get a well-balanced plate of scran. Forget eating five portions of fruit and veg a day; the brief lulls in fighting were usually spent gulping down ration packs, and, aside from hydration, our commanding officers rarely made a big deal about how we refuelled – it was all about quick fixes like energy bars, rehydration sachets and coffee shots. The food at base wasn't great either, and while we had access to protein, carbs and veg, it was rarely fresh. We would often try to sneak into the US Army's canteen because they had a decent salad bar.

I couldn't get my head around this set-up, because nutrition was massively important under such a physical workload. I'd also learned early on in my career that quick fixes could screw with an operator's performance levels. During Selection, on the Hills Phase, the lads pulled all sorts of tricks so that they could stay hydrated as we ran a series of time trials across the Brecon Beacons. Blokes were banging back the rehydration formulas, but a lot of them wilted in the heat because they'd made the mistake of taking on too many powdered drinks with not enough fluid. They then dropped like flies and failed the course. I nearly made the same error by necking a load of electrolytes the night before my final march. I woke up in the night feeling like death and the aching in my stomach lasted throughout the next day. Though I managed to finish the trial in time, it was a lesson learned.

Currently, nutrition is a major part of my job. I have to be physically in shape to work, which means I'm constantly assessing what I eat and drink. I've also found that having a good dietary programme serves as a powerful emotional anchor in phases of stress. Whenever there's a solid meal plan in place, plus a well-stocked fridge, I feel more in control emotionally, knowing that I'm not going to lose my edge down the line. The most important thing is to have an understanding of what I'm eating and when, and I always make a point of improving my nutritional systems in times of calm. That way, when the chaos kicks in once more, I can train my full attention on whatever's going on, knowing that I'm not going to neglect my health and fitness.

This tactic really came into focus while I was laid up with a broken leg. I couldn't exercise in a way that was going to maintain my sharpness and I stressed about whacking on the weight. In fact, for the first few weeks I could barely walk and I'd been prescribed OxyContin to manage the pain. Aside from the fact that it's a very addictive semi-synthetic opioid, one of its annoying side effects was constipation and I was backed up for several days, which made me feel even more terrible as I slobbed about on the sofa, unable to move. Thankfully, I had a good nutrition plan in place. Knowing I was getting the right foods and nutrients made me feel less uncertain about my recovery time, and emotionally I was able to maintain an even keel. With a solid nutritional foundation, my physical recovery and return to full fitness felt less of a grind once I was able to walk again.

TACTICAL BRIEFING: SET YOUR NUTRITION RULES

There are all sorts of ways to plan your nutrition. However, everyone is different and an eating routine that might enhance one person's performance could potentially wreck another's, due to the factors of metabolism, physical size and allergies, among other things. That's why there's very little point in me outlining the number of calories I consume daily, or my favourite types of lean protein. What works for me might have the opposite effect on you, so instead I'm going to give you a few guidelines to ensure that your nutrition can reach an elite level.

SCOFF THE RAINBOW

By that, I don't mean follow the advertising slogan set by a well-known brand of sweets. Instead, load your plate with healthy colour – greens, reds, yellows, orange; broccoli, tomatoes, peppers, carrots. By spending more time in the fruit and veg aisle of a supermarket than anywhere else, you're setting yourself up for success.

MAXIMIZE BREAKFAST

I've made a rule for myself that no matter where I am, I'll always eat a healthy and filling breakfast – unless I'm in the wild and it's physically impossible. The reason I prioritize this meal is so that I can set a positive intention for the whole day: if I can nail breakfast, I psychologically feel better about hitting my goals. Usually I'll have a bowl of porridge, then train, before drinking a protein shake. If I'm on a cheat day, I'll eat pancakes (the healthiest I can find) with (maybe) a side of bacon.

RUN AN ANNUAL NUTRITIONAL MOT

I recently had my first DNA test and it revealed that my body is best suited to a Mediterranean diet, which comprises vegetables, healthy fats like olive oil, nuts, seeds, fruit, and seafood and fish. Research has shown that eating these foods can assist in heart health and blood sugar levels, and possibly reduce the risk of Alzheimer's. You might need a different diet altogether. I won't sugar-coat the cost, though: a DNA test can be expensive – the ones I've gone for have set me back between £250 and £500. Health checks can be expensive too. However, if it means that I can remain at my optimum performance levels for longer, I consider it a price worth paying. I'll be taking an annual medical from now on.

⊖ THE LOOK FORWARD

Don't forget to hydrate. Not only can a lack of water lead to fatigue, an increased heart rate and heat cramps during exercise, but it also screws with an individual's performance levels. Nutritionists reckon we should drink around two or three litres of water a day (booze and caffeinated drinks don't count – sorry), but there are also foods that you can snack on to increase your hydration, including berries, spinach, carrots and oranges.

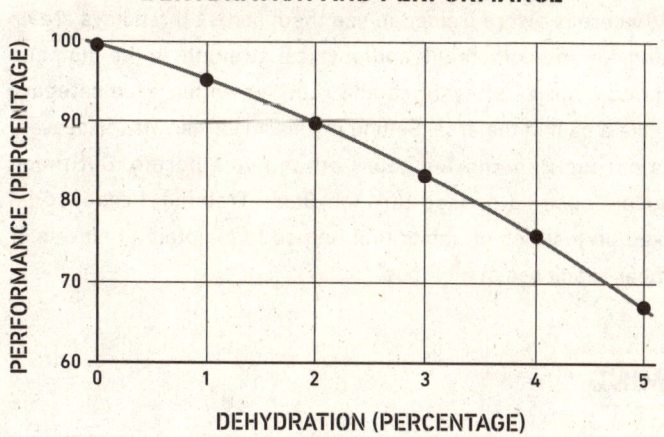

DEHYDRATION AND PERFORMANCE

CHAPTER 9
HABIT-BUILDING

Most of us are probably familiar with the concept of positive habits. In short, they're a series of acts that add to the quality of our lives and become ingrained in such a way that we feel bad if we're denied them. Sometimes, a positive habit becomes so routine that it happens almost without thought. Examples include:

- Checking in with a friend or family member every day.
- Having an alcohol-free week every month.
- Making a to-do list before going to bed.
- Putting a percentage of your salary into a savings account on payday.

My experience of adopting positive habits began in the military, where we were trained to use them across three keys areas: timing, kit and equipment, and physical strength. In the moment, building a series of systems and routines within each category felt like a pain in the arse. Setting my alarm earlier than necessary was boring. Running for hours on end was boring. But much later on, once I'd passed through Basic Training, I realized I'd picked up a series of habits that helped to maintain my levels of combat-readiness at all times.

TIMING

In war, timing was a matter of life and death. If you turned up late for a helicopter pick-up, the pilot was unlikely to hang around, burning fuel; he was probably going to disappear, because he was strategic-level transport, not a glorified Uber driver. (An Uber driver won't hang around for longer than five minutes, either.) As I said earlier, we were taught right from the off that to arrive on time was to be late, no matter what we were doing – briefings, training drills, meetings.

KIT AND EQUIPMENT

Being fastidious about kit maintenance was vital in order to get through Basic Training. That's why you'd never see a Marine come out of the field and say, 'Oh, I'll sort my kit later,' before disappearing for a shower and a kip. Instead, they'd immediately re-roll everything by replenishing the explosives and grenades, bombing up their magazines and clipping recharged batteries into various bits of equipment. Everything was then cleaned meticulously, before – *finally* – the Marine would look after himself by taking a shower and, if he was bloody lucky, getting his head down.

PHYSICAL STRENGTH

The importance of this is forced down a Royal Marine's throat. To get through Basic Training, an individual had to pass all sorts of tests, most of which involved gruelling physical exercise, and anyone who wasn't up to scratch was beasted. As with poor kit maintenance, a recruit who was unable to reach the highest standards of physical fitness was usually punished with extra push-ups, burpees and all sorts. It wasn't nice, but it was a bloody effective way of keeping the standards high.

The reason for this was simple: in battle, Commandos were expected to cover long distances and perform very physical tasks, such as scaling walls while carrying a heavy bergen. If they weren't able to do the job, there was a good chance they weren't going to make it home alive. This focus on physical fitness became even more acute for me later, in the military elite, where we were expected to be the best of the best in everything we did. It didn't help that some of our entry techniques could be bloody hard to execute. For example, I had one or two mates that were double fit – they were great soldiers, too – but for some reason they struggled whenever they were asked to make it on to a moving boat. If they fell off or screwed up, the old and bald would go mad, and send them off to the gym for extra strength-training. Their attitude: 'This is an asset you don't want moving on to a target because they'll be the first to die, which makes them a liability for the group as a whole.'

TECHNICAL BRIEFING: HACK THE HABIT LOOP

Building positive habits in the above three areas helped shape me as a soldier. However, the categories you personally decide to focus on might be totally different, so, in a period of calm, work out the ways in which your life might benefit from the addition of one or two productive routines. Then work on them. That way, they'll be ingrained by the time a new mission comes around, or when life turns hectic again. For example, you might be the owner of a small coffee shop, in which case try introducing positive habits into the following areas: your administration, product development and personal well-being.

Administration: Spend the first ten minutes of the day dealing with emails, tackling the most pressing ones first. Establish a to-do list for the day, ranking each task in order of importance.

Business Sustainability: Dedicate an hour or so a day to assessing your current financial position – with projections – and researching new ways of improving your business. Examples could include loyalty programmes (a free coffee for every ten purchases), a happy hour (half-price cakes) and social events (such as talks or group meetings).

Personal Well-Being: Incorporate positive habits to increase your health and happiness. In this case, the small-business owner might rely on exercise, social activities or time spent in nature to reduce their stress levels.

Once you've figured out the three key areas in which you'd like to incorporate a series of new routines, instil them with the 'habit loop' – a system introduced by Charles Duhigg in his book *The Power of Habit*, in which he describes how a habit is made up of three components: cue, routine and reward. Duhigg offers a case study of a negative cycle – a smoker who loves their after-dinner ciggy. The *cue* might happen at the end of a meal: the pushing away of the plate. The *routine* may involve the person going outside, opening the pack of cigarettes and sparking up. The *reward* is the rush of nicotine. Once these three actions have become psychologically linked, the brain creates a new neural pathway, fusing them together as a habit. In this case, every time the smoker finishes a meal, they immediately crave a cigarette.

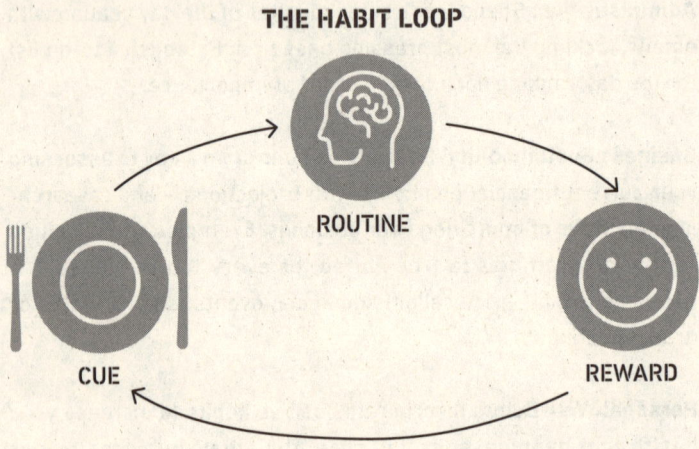

THE HABIT LOOP

ROUTINE

CUE

REWARD

But the good news is this process works for positive habits, too. We only need to create an enjoyable reward system that encourages us to do the tasks that might otherwise seem boring or unpleasant. So, the coffee shop owner might attach the following pleasurable activities to their cues and routines:

CUE	ROUTINE	REWARD
Morning	Sort emails	First coffee of the day
Lunchtime	Business research	Chat to customers
Evening	Tidy the premises	Walk home with friends

By attaching fun rewards to these otherwise boring – but important – tasks, the coffee shop owner will soon have adopted a series of positive habits. Not only will they help them to maximize their productivity, they'll also act as familiar processes for when life turns to shit. That, in itself, can create a sense of comfort.

⊕ THE LOOK FORWARD

Be prepared to grizz it out. Setting positive habits can be tough, especially if they involve doing something unpleasant such as taking a cold shower every morning. Currently, there are all sorts of ideas about how long it takes to make and break a habit. Some say twenty-one days, others argue for longer or shorter time frames, but given the variables in the play – such as the habit itself and the personality of the 'addict' – it's hard to know.

My experience of shivering through cold showers has revealed that, for me, a two-week stint is usually enough to lay down a mental marker – one that tells me I can cope with whatever habit I'm working on. But that's a personal response and everyone is different. For you, it might take more time, or less. Of course, the first few days of the showers were horrible, but by the beginning of the second week I started feeling OK. And after a full fortnight, my brain went from a sense of dread to a feeling of excitement as I cranked up the cold water. It also helped that the morning reward in my habit loop was a filling breakfast and the first coffee of the day. In those moments when the thought of a cold shower felt like torture, this acted as a powerful motivator.

CHAPTER 10
DIG INTO YOUR WEAKNESSES

In Episode One of the first series of *Special Forces: World's Toughest Test* (the American version of *SAS: Who Dares Wins*), a Directing Staff (DS) comprising Rudy Reyes, Mark 'Billy' Billingham, Remi Adeleke and me gathered together the celebrity recruits in a parade square. They were knackered, having been broken by a full day of running in the desert and 'tomb-stoning' from the side of a helicopter into the sea below. So, we decided to screw with their heads.

'Right, line yourselves up in the order of who you think is the weakest and the strongest.'

The recruits shuffled about, stepping into their positions from first to last. Some of them stepped confidently into the top positions – the NBA All-Star basketball player Dwight Howard took first place without evening thinking about it. The diminutive actress Beverley Mitchell anxiously put herself last. To be fair to her, she was being honest. Up until that point she'd done a good job of grabbing the bull by the arse in every task. She lacked confidence and common sense, and had rocked up on the first day wearing what looked like a pair of pyjamas. (She then had to crawl through the desert in them.) Dwight, on the other hand, while physically capable, had an ego the size of a house and everybody could see it.

The military often conduct self-assessments of this kind in training. Not to see who's the strongest or the weakest, but to assess which individuals might lack confidence and which ones have too much of it. An assessor will then tell each individual where they really are in the group, to bring a reality check to everyone involved, and we advanced this idea by getting the celebs to then walk a highwire that had been stretched across a canyon at a height of 100 metres. What happened next was fascinating. Dwight took an age to even step on to the line. He was a bag of nerves and fell almost immediately, before being caught by the safety line. Beverley, to everyone's surprise, made it nearly all the way across.

What had happened was that Dwight's strength and self-belief had become a weakness. By putting himself at the head of the pack, he suddenly found himself in a position where he had everything to lose. He then wilted at the first sign of pressure. Beverley, on the other hand, grew in stature because, by being honest about her position in the group, she had nothing to hide. Given she couldn't drop any further in the pecking order, Beverley threw caution to the wind and had a real go at the next test or two. *Her weakness had become a strength*. As a result, Beverley asserted herself in the next line-up and placed herself confidently in mid-table.

TACTICAL BRIEFING: TURN YOUR WEAKNESS INTO STRENGTH

We all have flaws and vulnerabilities; there's really no point in denying them, but sadly too many people do. They cover them up, fearful that other people will figure out their true personality, or realise that they're not as strong or capable as they might appear. As a result of this front, all sorts of toxic behaviour can spring up. We all know the traits: the teammate who bullies others to mask their own failures; the liar who can't tell their truth because it will bring out a past failure or moment of shame. But to truly grow, a person needs to perform a personal line-up of their own, like the one that took place in *Special Forces: World's Toughest Test*.

Of course, I'm not expecting you to stand in a line with your mates and figure out who's the strongest in the pack. But what I am urging you to do is to be honest about your weaknesses, because I promise you, once you do, your life will change for the better. My journey through PTSD is evidence of this. At first I denied that there was a problem and struggled to get well. It was only once I'd acknowledged I was in a bad way and needed help (and that it would be a slog to get better) that everything changed.

That process lasted all the way up to the writing of my first book, *Battle Scars*, which was a brutally open recollection of my struggles. Having read the book back to myself for the first time, I felt great about my recovery. But when I came to recording the audiobook, my perspective changed. Speaking the words aloud gave them a whole new power and I instantly felt exposed and anxious. I worried that everybody was going to hear my truth and think less of me because all my weaknesses had been laid bare. And then I realized that this was a positive step. On the book's release there was no hiding place any more and I could be my real self. *I had nothing to lose.* And that gave me strength.

⊕ THE LOOK FORWARD

Stand in the mirror and take a long look. Are you where you want to be in your life? Or are you masking some weakness or flaw? If the answer to the latter is 'yes', what can you do about it? This is the time to be painfully honest and open, though you don't have to share the things you think might need fixing with anyone else – not unless you want to. The important thing is self-assessment, without mercy, because that's where change can begin. Ignoring the process will only hold you back.

CHAPTER 11
DRAW YOUR PSYCHOLOGICAL TIMELINE

THE PSYCHOLOGICAL TIMELINE

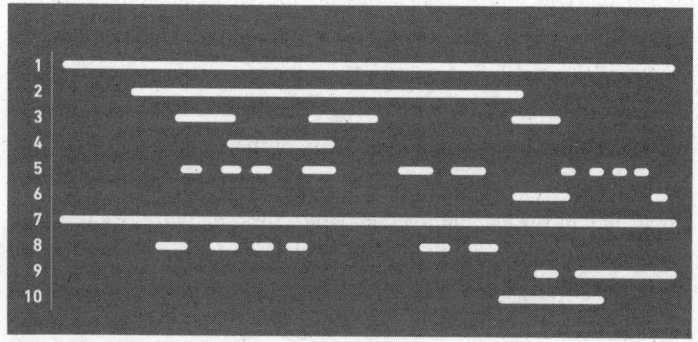

KEY   1 LIFE 2 MILITARY CAREER 3 CAREER COURSES 4 RELATIONSHIP DRAMA
5 DEPLOYMENTS/EXPEDITIONS 6 HEALTH 7 FAMILY 8 MOVING HOUSES, DOMESTIC
UPHEAVALS, ETC. 9 NEW CAREER 10 MILITARY CAREER-RELATED STRESS

As part of my mental health talks, I've recently encouraged my
audiences to consider what their 'Psychological Timeline' might
look like. This is a chart I've created for myself and it's made up of a
series of lines that run horizontally across a page, as shown in the
diagram. Some of the lines are continuous, others are broken up
like psychedelic Morse code, and each one represents an important
issue in my life, such as my career, expeditions, family, physical

and mental health and life itself. At the top of the graph is the 'life-line', starting from the day I was born and ending with the present. When examined as a whole, I can see exactly when I've been at my most stressed (it's in the sections of the chart when a high number of lines have run at once) and my happiest (where only a couple of lines are running).

By keeping an eye on these lines as I go forward, I can anticipate any future moments of stress. It's for that reason that the Psychological Timeline has become such an invaluable tool. In previous books and interviews, I've used the analogy of an overflowing pint glass to describe how I came to break down with PTSD. Back then, I explained how the glass began filling up with problems, one drop at a time, and for a while I was fine. But once my troubles had reached the brim and spilled all over the table, everything fell apart. Had I already devised the Psychological Timeline back then, there's a chance I could have known in advance that I was heading towards trouble.

The important thing with using data of this kind is that each line is written down without judgement or too much explanation. For example, one of my kids nearly died when she was born. While I know roughly where this event lands on the timeline (I can tell by looking at the dates), the lines aren't there to detail my emotions, because that's not the point of the graph. *I know I felt shit and overwhelmed back then.* Instead, the chart acts as an indicator of how my life has shaped up over time, while giving me an indication of what's going on in my present: if the lines are piling up on top of one another, I know that some corrective measures need to be taken. If not, I can relax.

TACTICAL BRIEFING: BREAKING DOWN YOUR LINES

When putting together a Psychological Timeline, it helps to think about the categories you'd like to include. This is a very personal choice, and no two graphs should look the same. For example, someone living with a chronic health condition will have a very different-looking set of categories from a person with zero health issues. To give you some pointers, here are a few of my categories.

LIFE

This runs from birth until the present day and it's a constant line that goes across the top of the page. Though all the big events appear in the categories below it, this line represents the background chatter that everyone deals with on a daily basis: relationships and marriages, exams, broken appliances, arguments with friends, the first day at work, bills, dentists' and doctors' appointments, and so on.

CAREER

It's in this section that I've charted my life with the Royal Marines and the military elite. There are breaks to indicate a) where I was medically discharged from the British Armed Forces and moved into a couple of civilian jobs, and b) the period I spent in therapy and recovery. Because of my TV work, it's been running steadily ever since.

HEALTH

This line includes my injuries, both physical and emotional, such as my breakdown and, later, my broken leg.

TOURS/EXPEDITIONS

The tours were moments of high stress, and when I was in the military they lasted anything from three to six months. Likewise, the expeditions: while being rewarding, there were occasions when I definitely thought my ticket was being punched.

FAMILY

We all experience unavoidable turbulence in this area. There are births and deaths, upheavals and disputes, kids and the responsibility of caring for them. But there are exciting moments, too, such as milestone birthdays, anniversaries and graduations, and these have to feature because this chart isn't designed to reflect only stress (though it can, if you like); it's to present every life event – good and bad.

Overall, this chart is an effective way of showing us that life is an unstoppable force. It keeps on going, no matter the size of our disasters – or successes. More importantly, the Psychological Timeline forces an individual to acknowledge everything that has taken place in their life. Too often people feel like shit and they're unable to work out why. By building a Psychological Timeline it's possible to see how the lines in your life have piled up or separated. After that, it's possible to understand clearly how, when and why your existence has been either hectic or tranquil.

⊕ THE LOOK FORWARD

Grab some coloured pens or pencils and practise drawing up your Psychological Timeline. Don't worry if it's not 100 per cent accurate on your first go – you can fully dig into the dates and more detailed events later on – but make sure to choose categories most applicable to you, then lay down the big events. Before long you'll have a clearer picture of when you felt calm and when you felt chaotic. By looking at what was going on in your life at those times, it's possible to figure out how many lines you should have running at once in order to feel in top condition.

CHAPTER 12
DREAM

In moments of calm, when there isn't a new project on the horizon or if I'm without a long-term mission to focus on, I'll take some time to dream about my future goals: what I'd like to do; where I want to go; who I want to go there with. It might sound a little lightweight, but there's no better way to locate a new challenge, or to shuffle through my priorities and figure out what the hell I want to do next. As I'm writing this, I'm in between seasons of *SAS: Who Dares Wins*. The producers recently asked me where I'd like the next series to be filmed, and what it should look like, and since then I've been running through different scenarios. In doing so, I've realized that I haven't spent enough time outdoors recently. I want to put myself in a position whereby I can move through an exciting environment without too much thought, other than the physical requirements needed to survive.

This sense of planning without boundaries keeps leading me to one type of location: a river, and a bloody big one, though I'm not sure exactly why. It might be because the big systems like the Amazon go on interesting journeys of their own, from source to mouth, and their personality changes along the way. Even though the waters of a large river are fairly still – that is, in comparison to a vast ocean like the Atlantic – negotiating one is still bloody hard work and absolutely terrifying at times. (As my experience traversing the Yukon rapids showed.) I'd love to do the Congo River, but that brings with it a shedload of risks, given it passes through one of the world's most violent places. The Amazon would be cool, but where does it even start? The more I think about it, the more I realize I'd like to travel the Mackenzie in the Canadian north-west, because it's over a thousand miles long and way more remote than the Yukon.

The process of assessing the future this way is both calming and relaxing. It takes me out of my head a little bit by distracting me from whatever else might be going on around me. Most of all it opens me up to new challenges and potential expedition ideas, triggering yet another mission cycle. I know a new period of chaos and effort isn't too far away – and I bloody love it.

TACTICAL BRIEFING: DREAM BIG

There's no point spending our downtime dreaming small, because it's in these moments that we should get lost in our ultimate ambitions, no matter how outrageous they may seem. As more than one successful entrepreneur has stated, 'If people aren't laughing at your ideas, then you're not thinking big enough.' I've taken that to mean that the people around me should be shocked at my future plans. My dad doubted me when I told him I was going to sign up with the Royal Marines. My mates laughed when I told them I was going to join the military elite. Before rowing the Atlantic and interviewing the most feared drug cartels in Mexico, I was told that I had a death wish. Those reactions showed me I was on the right path.

You should adopt the same mindset. Think big. *Bigger.* Give time and space to your dreaming, and when you do it, don't set any boundaries for what you hope to achieve. Conquer that physical challenge. Break new ground in your industry. Achieve your life-long ambitions. You don't believe you can do it? Fuck that: pretend that you can. And when people start taking the piss out of your ideas, take that as reassurance that you're thinking in the right way.

⊝ THE LOOK FORWARD

Set some time aside today to dream about your future goals. If you're stuck for inspiration, try some of the following questions as jumping-off points:

- What would your ultimate day look like?
- What were the ambitions of the teenage you?
- Close your eyes and stick a pin in a map: where are you going, what does it look like and how could you make it happen for real?
- Where do you want to be in one, five and ten years?
- You've come into some serious money. What do you do with it?

Then think big, without limits, and enjoy the experience. But most of all, *believe*.

CHAPTER 13
REMEMBER: YOU WILL DIE

Death is inevitable, but as far as I'm concerned, there's no point in fearing it. I'm cold and hard in that way, though I know that not everyone shares the same attitude. That said, I'm not ready to go just yet – there's so much more I want to achieve in life; but I do hope that one day I'll get to a stage where I feel comfy about slipping away, as some old people do. Recently, I started bringing up this subject at the very end of my speaking show. In the script, with the curtain about to drop, I've introduced the audience to the concept of *memento mori* – a Latin term that, when loosely translated, means 'remember you have to die'.

I'm sat in the Yukon River, having been chased from the bank by a grizzly bear. Sean and I deliberate for twenty minutes as to who's going to go in to pick up the rest of the kit. (In the end Sean did it.) A week later, we reach the Bering Sea and that's the end of our journey, in the same way that it's almost the end of our journey together here tonight. But before I go, I want to leave you with something that you can think about as you head home.

That something is memento mori.

Memento mori *is an old saying the Stoics once used as a reminder, a cue, to be aware of their own mortality. It's no secret that every day the sand drops through the hour glass of life and brings us a little closer to our meeting with the Grim Reaper. That's the bad news. The good news is that every day is a fresh start and at any point you can change your thinking and, as a result, the way you live your life. What you do is up to you. My change took place after the slow death of PTSD, when I decided to live the remainder of my life doing things that made me happy, things that brought out The Real Me. But life is about challenging yourself and finding what really makes you tick. It's also a short ride, so I dare you to go out there and find what your limit is. I genuinely hope that you never find it, that you keep pushing on, but in the process that you lead a life worth living . . .*

Rather than being a morbid thought, this term is intended to leave the watching punters with something inspirational, or to give them a boot up the arse. My aim is for it to have a similar effect on you.

Life is short.

Make the most of it.

Because failing to do so is the most terrifying reality of all.

TACTICAL BRIEFING: THE LIFE-EXPECTANCY CALCULATOR

The fact that we're all going to kick the bucket at some point isn't a cheery thought. However, it's probably the most motivational truth I can give you in this final chapter. The cold reality is this: *you will die*. Nobody lives for ever and time is bloody short, so make the most of it. Start that project. Make that life change. Cut out the bollocks excuses. Because otherwise, you're going to hit last orders without having made a difference and there's a good chance you'll feel pissed off about it.

If you want to get a sense of how much time you have left in which to achieve your goals, subtract your current age from the average life expectancy in the UK, which according to the Office for National Statistics is 79 years for males and 82.9 years for women. Then remember back to twelve months ago. *What was I doing? What were my plans? What have I achieved between then and now?* Bloody hell. That time flashed by quick, didn't it? And it's not going to slow down either, so get your arse into gear, switch on and make those changes today. You'll be thanking me by the time the final curtain comes down – if I'm still around to listen to you, that is.

⊖ THE LOOK FORWARD

Having used the life-expectancy calculator to work out how long you have left to live, statistically, really shake yourself up by throwing in some other life variables and check how much time you're wasting. For example, say you're a forty-year-old female who spends an hour a day on social media. Yes, you have 42.9 years of life left, but at the current rate, 15,658.5 hours of that limited time is going to be spent doomscrolling and/or gawping at Instagram, when you could be learning new skills, starting a business or doing anything else that might change your life for the better.

SO, WHAT ARE YOU WAITING FOR?

IT'S TIME TO LIVE LIKE YOU HAVEN'T GOT LONG LEFT . . .

RANDOMIZE
YOUR
CHALLENGE

As I stated in the introduction, this book can be read from cover to cover, or in segments. However, if you want to introduce a random element to the book, you can do so by **picking a card from a traditional playing deck** and taking on the relevant challenge as per the table on the following pages. My recommendation would be to **do one a week** so that you can test yourself for a full year ...

CLUBS

MISSION

DIAMONDS

RECOVERY

HEARTS

CHAOS

SPADES

CALM

YOUR 52 WEEKLY TASKS

PICK YOUR CARD AT RANDOM OR CHOOSE YOUR CHALLENGE FOR EACH WEEK

WEEK 1:

WEEK 2:

WEEK 3:

WEEK 4:

WEEK 5:

WEEK 6:

WEEK 7:

WEEK 8:

_____

_____

WEEK 9:

_____

_____

WEEK 10:

_____

_____

WEEK 11:

_____

_____

WEEK 12:

_____

_____

WEEK 13:

_____

_____

WEEK 14:

WEEK 15:

WEEK 16:

WEEK 17:

WEEK 18:

WEEK 19:

WEEK 20:

WEEK 21:

WEEK 22:

WEEK 23:

WEEK 24:

WEEK 25:

WEEK 26:

WEEK 27:

WEEK 28:

WEEK 29:

WEEK 30:

WEEK 31:

WEEK 32:

WEEK 33:

WEEK 34:

WEEK 35:

WEEK 36:

WEEK 37:

WEEK 38:

WEEK 39:

WEEK 40:

WEEK 41:

WEEK 42:

WEEK 43:

WEEK 44:

WEEK 45:

WEEK 46:

WEEK 47:

WEEK 48:

WEEK 49:

WEEK 50:

WEEK 51:

WEEK 52:

CREDITS

p. 17: Ikigai diagram. Source: Marc Winn (first published in the *Toronto Star*, 14 May 2014).

p. 22: Facing your fears diagram. Source: https://www.dummies.com/article/body-mind-spirit/emotional-health-psychology/psychology/cognitive-behavioral-therapy/facing-your-fears-with-cognitive-behavioural-therapy-267181/

p. 50: Stress curve diagram. Source: https://www.scienceofpeople.com/psyched-up/

p. 61: Reward–compulsion loop diagram. Source: https://www.smeweb.com/wp-content/uploads/2019/08/One4all-Rewards-Compulsion-Loop.png

p. 122: Danger of overworking diagram. Source: Leger, D. *Sleep*, 17, pp. 84–93 (1994). https://www.nature.com/articles/40775

p. 217: Circadian rhythm cycle diagram. Source: NobelPrize.org. Nobel Media AB 2021. https://www.nobelprize.org/prizes/medicine/2017/press-release/

p 237: Dehydration and performance diagram. Source: https://pressbooks.bccampus.ca/nutr1100/chapter/keeping-fit-the-benefits-of-physical-activity/

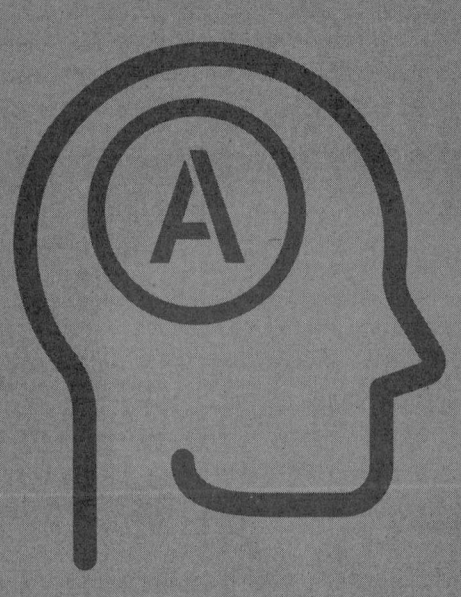

ACKNOWLEDGEMENTS

If you have read my previous books, *Battle Scars* and *Life Under Fire*, you will understand that it has taken a long time and a lot of hard experience to earn the perspective and clarity that I have today, all of which I have channelled into *Embrace the Chaos*. Fortunately, it has not been a journey I have taken on my own.

This book is dedicated to my parents, Peter and Hilary. I must thank them for their enduring support and for the values they instilled into my brothers and me from an early age. They have faced the triumphs and disasters of life with courage, determination, unselfishness and cheerfulness. I would later come to recognize these as the four pillars of the commando spirit, but they have always been the cornerstones of my life.

Special mention must go to my wife, Jules, for truly embracing my chaos, as well as to my two brothers, Mat and Jamie, and to my expanding Brotherhood from the military and beyond. We might be a ragtag bunch, but our community has held me up when needed and has helped me to find my purpose. We are all stronger together.

This book would not have been possible without a few key individuals. Cheers to everyone at M&C Saatchi Merlin, particularly Emily Rees Jones, Lucy Kilner and Lily Wilde. Thanks also to the team at Transworld and Penguin Random House, particularly Barbara Thompson, Thomas Hill, Rosie Ainsworth and my editor, Henry Vines. Finally, I must thank my writing partner, Matt Allen, without whom this book simply wouldn't exist.

Foxy
London, 2024

ABOUT THE AUTHOR

JASON FOX joined the Royal Marine Commandos at sixteen, serving for ten years, after which he passed the gruelling selection process for the Special Forces, serving with the Special Boat Service for over a decade.

Today, you are most likely to find him gracing our television screens and giving us a taste of action and adventure around the world. He is the author of two bestselling books, *Battle Scars* and *Life Under Fire*.

Also by Jason Fox

Battle Scars
Life Under Fire